# OBJECT · PAINTING

*Robert Ryman,* Surface Veil, *1970, oil on plexiglass with wax paper frame and tape, 56x48cm (reproduced courtesy of Pace Wildenstein, New York)*

# OBJECT · PAINTING

Andrew Benjamin

**A.D.** ACADEMY EDITIONS

Acknowledgements
I have been fortunate in being able to present drafts of these chapters as lectures in a number of different places. Consequently I would like to thank the staff and students at the following institutions for the help and stimulus they provided: The Humanities Centre, Cornell University; Wimbledon School of Art; Department of Fine Art, University of Leeds; Department of Philosophy, State University of New York at Stony Brook; School of Architecture, Columbia University; Tate Gallery, London. In addition I would like to thank those with whom I have discussed the project undertaken here: Christine Battersby, Peter Osborne, Tim Murray, Greg Lynn, Stan Allen and Hugh Silverman. I would also like to thank Simon Sparks for helping me prepare the manuscript, Vivian Constantinopoulos in the early stages, and Nicola Hodges who is all and more one could ever want in an editor.

Andrew Benjamin

Jacket illustration: Christian Boltanski, *Les Suisses morts*, 1990, black and white photographs, metal lamps, installation view, Institute of Contemporary Art, Nagoya, 1990 (reproduced courtesy of Lisson Gallery, London)

First published in Great Britain in 1994 by
ACADEMY EDITIONS
an imprint of the Academy Group Ltd

ACADEMY GROUP LTD
42 Leinster Gardens London W2 3AN
Member of the VCH Publishing Group

ISBN: 1 85490 361 6

Copyright © 1994 Andrew Benjamin

Distributed to the trade in the United States of America by
ST MARTIN'S PRESS
175 Fifth Avenue, New York, NY 10010

Printed and bound in Italy

# CONTENTS

*Langlands & Bell*, Adjoining Rooms, *1989, beech, MDF, glass, perspex, AC lacquer, 78x426x62cm (reproduced courtesy of Glenn Scott Wright, Contemporary Art)*

# Introduction

*... il faut continuer, je ne peux pas continuer, je vais continuer.*
**Samuel Beckett, *L'Innommable***

Philosophy has always concerned itself with art. Within any history of philosophy the attempt by philosophy to address the nature of art must occupy a major role. Consequently, any undertaking to renew this relation will have to accept and thus must work with these already present determinations. While art is restricted in this context to installations and painting, with the existence of an already present relation, the question that must inevitably emerge touches on how a response to the given is to be taken up and thus presented. Responding systematically to philosophy's already present attempts to establish a relation to art will, in this instance, not take a high priority. What will be of central concern here, however, is presenting the possibility of an-other philosophical thinking about art.[1] As always the question that arises is the nature of alterity. What will characterise and mark out the otherness of this 'other thinking'? The provisional answer is that it will be determined by the type of relation that is envisaged with what is already present; with tradition understood as the work of the already given.[2] The rationale for such an undertaking, it will be argued, lies in the particularity of the art object itself. Part of the project that will be developed, therefore, will concern tracing and developing this particular construal of the art work. What was once taken as unproblematic, namely the presence of a given object, will, in the following chapters, come to be repositioned in terms of art work. And yet art work is not a description of an object at rest. On the contrary art work is the work — the action — proper to art. It will be with the move to work and with it to process that it will become possible to take up the question of the object that will, in its effectuation, differentiate itself from the usual philosophical construals of the object.

## Tracking, Tacking

As a way in two interrelated yet different movements will be necessary. They will work within each other, opening up the possibility of the complex interplay of affirmation and differentiation that will work to distance the certainty provided by tradition's repetition. 'Tracking' and 'tacking' refer to complex and varied movements. Tracking involves following paths that are only barely present; pursuing traces, moving ahead via information rather than following the predicted route opened by certainty. Tacking is a means of accepting the given — engagement's site — without taking over the totality in which it is given. Tracking aims to complete but by inventing. Tracking entails responding to hints and therefore to another listening. Tracking is neither the work of prediction nor of pure speculation; the latter being a futural opening marked by the envisaged absence of constraints. Tacking, however, will allow for the possibility of a productive move that takes over, but without allowing that which is taken over to dominate. Here, in order to attempt to take up the question of the art object, as a question, and the presence of installations and painting, as fields of work, from within philosophy (from within philosophy while reworking that project and thereby not simply repeating philosophy's worn determinations) both these forms of movement will be necessary.

Prior to pursuing their work, what must be noted in passing is that while both involve different, though related, ways of resisting the given and therefore the determinations guiding philosophy's already existent attempts to incorporate art, they are fuelled, nonetheless, by a commitment to a precise construal of the ontological nature of art work. This commitment involves a number of different elements. The first is that this conception of the art object is both insistently and effectively present. In other words ontological considerations form an ineliminable part of the object's presence. The second is that part of what marks out the work of tradition is the incorporation of art into the problematic of representation, denying thereby what defines the specificity of art work, namely the continuity of its becoming. As will be seen, it is this continuity which will allow the reworking of the art work (or art object) in terms of what will be identified as the *becoming-object*. Finally, therefore, because tradition has always attempted to efface that which is proper to art work — namely the continuity of becoming — working through the determinations of tradition in order to release and thereby affirm the hold of becoming will demand the copresence of affirmation and differentiation. Engaging with the given and thus with that which continues to give itself as the work of tradition, present as the logic of the gift, will mean that the movement of engagement and distancing will need to be taken up.[3] Part of such an undertaking will depend upon the recognition that the interplay of engagement and distancing — an interplay that will also involve 'working through' the given — occurs simultaneously. It is not as though one is a precondition for the other; rather, it is with this twofold movement occurring at the same time that tracking and tacking come to be connected. While tacking is another description of the difficult process of working through the already given, the strategy of movement will not follow what is merely given. And yet what is given is not to be understood as an obstacle whose force can be simply displaced, destroyed or forgotten. Metaphysical destruction will not play a role here. If there is an adequate image, then both taking the already given as a force, and recognising that working through that force is an inescapable necessity, will mean that the given should be allowed the presence of a headwind. It should be noticed, again in passing, that the time of this *at the same time*, the time of engagement and distancing, forms part of the complex temporality of interpretation. While it will be essential to return to this time what insists at this stage is movement.

Part of this movement's complexity is its fragility. Tacking is the difficult movement forward that will demand constant attention and care, for at any moment the prevailing wind may upset and cause the movement of engagement and distancing to founder.

Tacking takes the presence of work as ineliminable. Tacking is a working against that does not hover in the space of impossibility; other tracks will have emerged instead. Tacking, therefore, is a process that resists accepting as final the work of negation on the one hand, and concluding with the lament of the aporetic on the other. Distancing this lament is equally a distancing of the *via negativa* that only opens up once impossibility and the negative become ends in themselves. The way indicated by these complex movements will always be determined by an insistent affirmation. Countering the work of negation — a countering that marks the limits of the negative — means plotting an-other way. Tacking therefore becomes a way of marking out the abeyance of predication which in turn opens up the affirmed presence of the strategic; strategies yielding different ways. With the strategic, chance may come to play an important role.[4]

It may seem, however, that the evocation of chance would itself be undermined by the assertion of an actual ontology of the art object, since attributing a necessary and fixed quality would engender the work of necessity rather than the unfolding of chance. Nonetheless it is the actual nature of the object that precludes this from being the case; and it is this point that must be pursued. Chance and contingency, once they are incorporated within an opposition in which their opposed possibilities are reason and necessity, only ever function as a threat whose probable actualisation is already overcome. They are no threat because of their place within a pregiven opposition. In this sense, therefore, chance is not subject to the work of chance and contingency is never contingent. Their presence within the opposition that provides the specificity of their place means that both are already part of a necessary determination. Here, rather than locating chance within an already positioned opposition, it is replaced and thus reworked. The relation to the art object must be taken as having this initial setup, as deploying this other chance; furthermore, what must also be retained is the nature of the attempt being undertaken here, namely to occasion an-other philosophical thinking about art. Part of what defines the alterity in question is a move away from an ontology of substance or essence and towards an ontology of becoming in which what is fundamental to the work *is* its work. It will be work, coupled with a specific form of questioning, that will define the nature of the object, and in so doing will situate chance. What is meant by questioning here, while always having a precise and therefore regional determination, nonetheless allows itself a specific generality.

The generality in question is the claim that what characterises the art object is that it incorporates, as part of its work, its raising and maintaining the question of what an art object is. (In continually enacting the question of the object, it comes to take on the quality of what will be described as the *object-in-question*.) Work therefore incorporates the ontology of becoming in which there is a continual giving and the temporality of the question in which the work's work is maintained by its opening up the space of the question. The question in being a question, and therefore in being retained as a question, works — temporally — to resist the possibility of an enforced closure. Finally, while this tentative outline of the nature of the object involves a clear commitment to a form of necessity because of the interplay of questioning and becoming, the regional presence of this general setup cannot be presented in advance. Moreover, because there has been a displacing of this interplay within philosophy's traditional take on art, uncovering, showing and thus affirming its presence will demand moves that involve a reciprocal, though now complex, displacement. Part of what this entails is the use of procedures — be they interpretive or experimental — that in taking over the given repositions and reworks it beyond tradition's own hold. An envisaged relation of non-relation enacts conceptions of chance and the strategic that are no longer simply the op-posite of necessity and reason.

### Via Negativa

Part of any adventure must be a conception of the place of departure and, with that, the relationship between the construal of that place and the nature of the task at hand. While it is always possible to describe the place in generic terms and thus deploy uncritically formulations such as modernism or post-modernism, a more general description can be given by utilising the term 'present'. What this will mean is that the varying formulations of modernism, post-modernism etc, all become descriptions of the contemporary site of understanding and activity. While the site and the varying activities will bear the same date, the present is itself to be understood as the topos incorporating claims that seek to identify the contemporary. As each description generates a particular task — the consequences for action in taking the present in one specific way — and since the tasks, as with the conceptions of the present themselves, will generate an internal conflict, the present, understood as a generalised topos, becomes the site of conflict over its own identity. In other words what will be named by the present, used in this general sense, is the conflict within it, in order to identify the contemporary with that which would amount to only one particular formulation of the contemporary. Within this setup one possible construal of the present works within the way opened up by an insistence on negativity, impossibility and the aporetic. It is important to take the generalised work of the negative as a description of the present, as what this work announces is a necessary determination of philosophical and interpretive tasks. Intruding here is already to intrude within the conflict concerning the present; and even while conceding the inescapability of intrusion it is still possible to suggest that what the via negativa resists is the possibility of an-other thinking of transformation. The negative here must be understood, in part, as that thinking which precludes the intrusive and originating presence of the work of repetition.

Repetition stands opposed to negation. And yet repetition is not in opposition to negation. It is not negation's negation. An integral part of this negativity — recognising immediately the problem of generalisation — is that the present is marked out as a site of irreconcilability gesturing towards a future reconciliation; or the present becomes the place in which there is an insistence upon the impossibility of project as an end in itself; or the present is given by the presence of an insisting melancholia precluding and therefore resisting work. Countering these determinations, all of which preclude the possibility that repetition (what will be an-other repetition) may play a constitutive role within the present, means accepting the need to continue and, therefore, taking up the question of how to go on becomes part of the task at the present; this present. What arises here, with this present, is the question of the future. How is it possible to allow the future to form an integral part of the present? In outline it is because the present is always produced. Even in those positions which posit the present as part of an essential continuity it can be argued that the present is produced by a repetition of the Same. It is the Same which takes place. Production will always involve work, and part of this work will involve working with the given; working with that which is already given. Insisting on production will mean that the present is a site of activity (maintaining the level of generality it is possible to argue that conflict needs to be understood on the level of action) that is positioned by repetition. Displacing the hold of the negative entails allowing for an-other repetition. It is this possibility that here is either located in works — located as affirmatively present — or deployed in the interpretation of works.

Repetition thought of as a productive possibility that while sanctioned by the ontology of the art object — ontology understood in terms of the becoming-object — overcomes the work of the negative by allowing for a present in which the repetition of the Same gives way to other possibilities. It will be this form of repetition that demands the primordiality of relation and allows for differentiation and thus difference to emerge in terms of the work of the logic of the apart/a part and the again and anew. Both of these procedures which will be formulated in detail in the following chapters, will be presented in terms of their productive presence within the analysis of painting and objects to come.

*Jenny Holzer, selections from* Truisms *(1986-7): Dupont Circle, Washington DC (above); Candlestick Park, San Francisco (below) (reproduced courtesy of Barbara Gladstone Gallery, New York)*

# Objects and Questions

Today the question of the art object seems a distant concern. The developments within the visual arts, plus what is often taken to be the gradual erosion of any sustained distinction between what has come to be identified as 'high and low art', have worked to distance the question of the art object. It is as though these developments have rendered such questions redundant. They may have become untimely or, at the very least, out of place with a certain presentation of historical time. There are however a number of difficulties in attempting, finally, to rid writing on art of the necessity to return to the question of the object. Here, rather than isolating these difficulties and then working back through them, another approach will need to be taken. There will need to be another way of beginning. Consequently, as a prelude, the form and the formulations that characterise this approach will be set out. Within it — with the approach's actual unfolding — the question of the object will come to emerge in a different way; a way that will avoid the simple positing of the object. The overall claim to be developed and sustained in the proceeding is that once art is understood in terms of *movement*, a movement that is internal to the frame, internal though incorporating framing as a device integral to the art work's being, emphasis will then come to be placed on the work. Work however will, in the process, lose its substantive and thus static quality. Arising from this loss — a loss that has of course the characteristics of an overcoming — will be this other possibility. What differentiates it from other approaches is that it makes the work's 'work' central, if not essential.

The movement from work both construed and located within an ontology of stasis towards work taken as an activity, in opening up the actative in lieu of the substantive, repositions, or perhaps reworks, the ontology of the art object in terms of becoming.[1] Within what will have been opened by this reworking and thus with the envisaged centrality of becoming (therefore with what will come to be identified as the becoming-object), art will inevitably be concerned with the question of its own objectivity and thus with its own being as art. The question, of course, is the question of that being. How is the being in question to be thought? In sum, what will be at stake is the object understood as the becoming-object of the work of art. By repositioning the question of the ontology of the art object it will become impossible — except through the nihilism of a staged and deliberate forgetting — to avoid the question of the object, since the consequence of that repositioning is that art continues, as part of its work and as part of its being art, to address the question of its being. In other words it will emerge that it is only by retaining the centrality of ontology, albeit a differential ontology, that the propriety of the object can be located. Furthermore, it will be within the process that allows for the relocation of propriety that the art object is itself being repositioned beyond the determinations set by a philosophy of the essence. Before this position can be reached — in other words attained rather than merely either identified or posited — a start needs to be made. Here the point of departure will concern what is already at work. Even though its work can only be noted retroactively, a beginning can be made with the insistent presence of the art object. Art is already present. The already identified presence of art will open, if only initially, the question of the object. Responding to that question, here, would be linked not only to the necessity — a necessity enjoining a type of obligation — to take up the question of the object, but more insistently to what will emerge as the ontology of the art object. Ontology and signification will be interconnected in the object's work.

One of the reasons why it is difficult to avoid art's own insistent presence pertains to what remains as a continual and emphatic element in contemporary developments within art practices; in other words within the activity of art itself. It is however a presence often obscured in the attempt to eliminate questions concerning the object. What endures as present, and moreover as effectively present, is the residual defining link, albeit a negative link, to purpose and thus to function. Art's relation to the question of function endures. Even within the parameters set by a distancing of the high/low distinction, as well as with the incorporation of dimensions which do not 'standardly' pertain to questions concerning the art object, there remains as both necessary and productive the turn from the possibility of purpose and with it the essential eschewing of function. Putting this more accurately it can be suggested that what endures is a construal of art as the self-regulating, and thus as prescribing an internality that in turning from the possibility of utility has to regulate itself. As a beginning it can be argued that art is present as that which has both a self-given purpose and a self-defined function; autonomy in its most elementary form. It will be in this precise sense that art sets for itself its own purpose and its function — and here function must be taken beyond the range of utility, eg art functioning as propaganda. The purpose and function in question is to be art. And yet this statement at this stage is no more than a tautology. It demands to be developed. Development however will need its own place and thus its own location. Rather than offering a setting that is either historical or social — a possibility precluded by what here is being essayed — the setting will have to be thought philosophically. What that will demand is the taking up of an inscription that can neither be avoided nor refused, and which therefore in its determining presence sets up the conditions of possibility for meaning, understanding and experience. The already given — the determination of the already given, its work — is *tradition*. It is the site of an ineliminable inscription. Art is always inscribed within the work of tradition, just as it has that work inscribed within it.[2] The possibility of autonomy will need to be understood in relation to the inescapable presence of tradition; tradition's repetition. It will be essential to maintain the link — what may in the end be the burden of the link — to tradition. Relation's insistence and the link with tradition will necessitate that destruction and the new take on determinations which are no longer formulated within a metaphysics of destruction.[3] One direct consequence of this is that autonomy will have to be reconsidered firstly within the terms set by the primordiality of relation and secondly in connection to the ineliminable presence of repetition. Maintaining the link with tradition will also entail that the temporality within which tradition is traditionally conceived will have to be shown as necessarily connected to tradition's work. A further consequence will therefore be that a fundamental part of the displacing of tradition's work will be the displacing and replacing of this temporality. Both have to be undertaken if the art object is to be taken up in terms of work and the actative. In the end, all these considerations will come to be interarticulated and thus are to be taken as central to an understanding of art's work.

Here the question of being — being art — if it is assumed as already answered, retains the question of the object, but as closed off. If the question is retained as a question and thus the art's work (the art work as the site of a productive process) is understood as maintaining that question as a question — allowing a certain regionalism and a necessary and therefore ineliminable specificity within the question — then what must emerge is an opening. The opening, however, will need to be thought of as much temporally as spatially. The interpretive response to that opening will be the necessity of tracing the various ways in which the question of the object will have been retained as a question. Part of this project will involve indicating that if within the activity of interpretation the question is able to endure as a question (a question within and as part of the work's own work) it is then possible for art to have a critical and thus political dimension. The point of such an undertaking will be to redirect a thinking of art away from the *via negativa* that characterises the conception of modernity which yields, from within its own encounter of the aporetic, the philosophical and artistic project of post-modernism, and therefore towards what may lay claim to another modernity.[4] Initially the problem will be how this alterity — the other in question — is itself to be understood. What would the other modernity be? Part of the answer will involve a specific claim about the work of art and, with it, what establishes the specificity of art work. Even though the detail of the answer will always need to emerge from an analysis of specific works — an analysis of the work as work — it remains the case that what can be noted in advance is that a significant element of any answer will involve a distinction that can be drawn between different forms of presence. Not all art works in the same way even though all may be art works. The detail of this difference will itself be explicable in terms of affirmation. The complexity of affirmation is that, in being linked to the determinations of historical time, it will sanction the reworking and, as a consequence of that act, the reintroduction — present however as an-other repetition — of the question of value.

With this opening, what has already emerged are a number of areas of inquiry. Central to each is the nature of art's presence and either an explicit or implicit reference to time. The place of the art work will be inextricably connected to the time in which it takes place; the time of its being present, its being at the present. The time in question is not to be explained in terms of the time of dates — a time the progression of which conflates a hitherto generalised time and chronology — nor, moreover, is it explicable in terms of the temporal hold of genre; the time of genre. The latter being those periods of time which in being given names work by virtue of that gift to name; and, in naming, then to hold within the period what it is that takes place within the unfolding of the period in question (taking place can have either a negative or positive sense). It goes without saying that there is an interdependency here insofar as the time of genre will depend upon dating to fix borders and determine the confines of the so-called period in question. Part of the consequences of the argument being presented and the analyses to be presented here will be the possibility of being able to release art works from the hold of this conception of history. (It will be a possibility traversed by necessity.)[5]

The release involves a certain complexity. As a start the release, while sanctioned by the ontology of the art object, is nonetheless a possibility that is enacted within (and as) interpretation. (At work here is an approach other than a simple hermeneutic, the most telling reason why is that what can be taken as the temporality of interpretation is itself already radically distinct from the implicit temporality of genre.) In being released the works are no longer committed to the hold of the generic and can, as a result, come to play a role and be allowed to be at work in the present. The present understood as the time constructed by the purpose of a particular task will allow for the reintroduction of purpose; a reintroduction that marks the presence of purpose's own reworking. Art works' relevance and constitutive place within the present (this present) therefore will depend upon the growing irrelevance of tradition's hold. The nature of this other work — art's work — is explicable in terms of its relation to repetition. Tradition's presence will need to be understood as a repetition. The conflict engendered by the interplay of relevance and irrelevance will involve the possibility of another repetition. It will be the sundering of tradition's hold — tradition as the repetition of the Same — that attests to the critical potential within art. Furthermore it will be a sundering whose identification joins art and the practice of criticism, allowing, if necessary, a distinction between criticism and mere historical commentary. And finally it will be a sundering that is itself made possible by what is unique to the art work, though more specifically in what can be identified as specific to the work's work. Emphasising work will be part of what causes and allows the object to be given an-other description. Further work — and therefore furthering work — is the activity of interpretation.

## To Work

If only as a point of departure a start can be made with work and thus with a work. Jenny Holzer's neon signs flash; their content — and their conditions of possibility — figuring in the flashing of lights and the work of illumination. Their position — the installed *Truisms* — the actual site in which they figure, gives to the signs an important regional force. The eye is drawn, at least initially, to the overall field of coloured lights and with them to their display. With that drawing display will open as a question. The lights, even though they are given, are not static. They do not provide a simple space of contemplation. In their movement, in their repetition, the relationship between the spectacle and capitalism is repeatedly framed; the same force is continually reframed. It is precisely this context that provides Holzer's work with its regional force, its site of intervention and with it of critique. The work has a specific site. It is therefore — and with all the complexity that will be able to be given to the term — site-specific. And yet what must still endure as a field of inquiry is how that specificity is both provided and maintained. Why are these *Truisms* not assimilated? How are they held a part from the spectacle? Why are they more than information? In sum, why are they are not absorbed into the popular cultural form of advertising on which they depend?

Answering these questions will work to open up the question of the object and as a result it will be the movement of that work which will have to be pursued. Moreover the answers to the questions pertaining to *Truisms* will themselves work to indicate that what endures as a productive force is the object. However what will arise as present within the works under consideration here is not the object itself, as if there were a simple object existing as 'itself', but the continual questioning of the object. In other words there is the sustained presence of a work, part of whose work is to raise and maintain the question of the object; as will be suggested what this will mean is that once questioning is allowed to play a dominant role in the conception of the object, then, rather than just repeating that the area of concern is the object, the object should be re-expressed as the object-in-question. (While this will be presented in greater detail it should already be clear that the formulations *becoming-object* and the *object-in-question* are themselves ways of signalling that a repositioning and reworking of the object is taking place.) With the presence of this setup two of its integral components need to be identified. The first is that with it there is an-other take on questioning. The second is that what arises with this opening is that the art object will be able to sustain a critical dimension by bringing art's determinant relationship with its own history into play. Critique will reinscribe the possibility of a politics of arts that henceforth will take place beyond the simple evocation of a triumphant assertivism. (While it may seem distant from these provisional formulations, what will emerge is that understanding the way in which critique arises will itself depend upon reworking the nature of the relationship between art and time.)

With the work *Truisms* — with its work — lights move. They appear, forming part of a generalised display; not just a part but, more emphatically, an integral part of the whole. What the setting displays is the inescapable link between information and the commodity. Even the flashing sign conveying time, perhaps the one with the brief display of news items, works to turn information into part of a generalised display of what is able to be consumed. Information and consumption operate beyond the purview of anything that could be described in terms of advertising. (This 'beyond', while a real possibility, will itself need to be questioned.) The *Truisms* are there within that setting. Their initial hold will always need to be given in terms of that within which they form a part. As part of it they refer to it. Formally they seem integrated into it. It is thus that the question of assimilation returns. While it is perhaps clear how they form a part, the question of how they remain apart still persists. Taking up this latter question will have to begin with the recognition that their being held apart cannot be separated from any account of how they form a part of the more generalised site. Indeed it will be possible to go further and suggest that one will depend on the other. It will be the articulation of this work within terms set by what will be called the logic of a part/apart that will account for the work's work while at the same time indicating why the presence of the art object is raised, and raised more emphatically, by the work of this logic. What must be taken up therefore is the straightforward way in which a constructive parasitism provides these works with their work. Emphasis must be given to work and thus to the work's work. By concentrating on work and thus on what is best described as the actative dimension within art works, be they paintings, sculptures or installations, there will be an important addition. However, it will not figure as an additional element.

Emphasising work and with it the productive nature of the object — the becoming-object, the productive movement therefore of its becoming — will mean that central to any understanding of the object will be time. Allowing for the centrality of time will mean that the assumed dominant significance of space will have yielded its place to time. Pursuing the apart/a part, and thus this work's founding parasitism, will be that which causes the already present work of time to open up. As a beginning, however, what must be identified is a provisional description of both parasite and parasitism. Clarification is needed in advance. In sum, parasitism involves a complex relation in which there is a necessary dependency. The parasite depends upon the host and in certain cases the host may, in a certain limited sense, depend upon the parasite. The difference is that the parasite owes its existence to the host. One intriguing consequence of this dependence is that the parasite could never take the place of the host. It could not be the host; in other words it could not host itself. What is parasitic is almost definitionally apart while being a part. Because of this placing, if there were a logic of parasitism then it would have to operate in terms of a necessary but more significantly constitutive disequilibrium. Nonetheless what characterises this relation — a relation perhaps best described in terms of an unequal dependence — is that it does not involve negation. Negation will not be significantly complex. It is this aspect of the logic of the a part/apart that will have to be pursued.

There will be two senses in which it will be possible to identify the work of this logic. (These two different senses may, of course, intersect within the work of specific works.) The first involves the relation between art and non-art, while the second is the incorporation of a genre that, while present within the frame, does not dominate it. Moreover, in the second, the opening allowed by the apart/a part will become the locus of the work's own engagement with the tradition it incorporates. In neither case will the division be either exact or absolute; there will be points at which there is a flow between them. The separation is not intended to be absolute; and yet there is a separation (it is as though the differentiation is at the same time concise and fuzzy). All examples become therefore the affirmation of the primordiality of relation. With Holzer's *Truisms* the obvious and unavoidable question would concern why it is that these works are not drawn back into the background thereby becoming part of an undifferentiated urban landscape of light and display. There will always be this risk because the works utilise the medium of advertising; indeed it should be noted in passing that it is the presence of this risk, both an unavoidable and a necessary risk, that yields an internal criterion of assessment. The question of relation still insists. Initially the *Truisms* attract because they seem to be just another way of employing the means of advertising; popular culture in its differentiation from art work. While the works in question employ those means they are not reducible to the operation of advertising and thus are not an instance of the simple repetition of those means. (There is a repetition, however its operation is far more complex.) The irreducibil-ity in which this complex repetition figures is an integral part of the work's work. Furthermore that which constructs and maintains the irreducible is the presence of what allows the site to exist as such in the first place; again, this is the effective presence of repetition. In other words the impossibility of a reduction either to the work of art in its absolute differentiation or the work of advertising in its complete separation from any other possibility is the consequence of the original dependence. The means of advertis-ing and thus of non-art have to be maintained in order that what is present is, in its dependency on it, not reducible to it. The work's work has to involve both elements. Being apart from it is itself only possible because of its being a part of it. The presence of non-art is not negated; indeed it is put to work.

This point can be reinforced and developed by incorporating repetition into the link between work and time. It will be this link that will allow the question of the ontology of the art work — the object's being — to be brought to the fore. What will emerge is that construal of the object in which it is presented as being-at-work. (It will be due to the nature and centrality of work coupled with the interarticulation of work and ontology that this being will find expression in terms of the becoming-object or the object-in-question.) The irreducibility that is marked out by the a part/apart occurs at the same time; the task is taking up this time. At the same moment there is the repetition of the means of advertising which in its not repeating all the determinations of those means holds open the work — a holding that is the mark of an ineliminable irreducibility. Specifying the place of this work will involve a description of how the irreducibility figures since the work's work occurs in, and with, that opening. The moment in which an anoriginal plurality is to be sited and therefore the time that is the 'same time' at which the constitutive elements of the apart/a part pertain is complex from the start — it is thus an event; also the complexity and hence its status as an event is only recoverable retroactively, and therefore within the constitutive movement of interpretation. The latter point indicates that interpretation has to be given its own temporal determinations (these determinations themselves to be thought through a reworking of the Freudian conception of *Nachträglichkeit*[6]). The productive interplay of repetition and a constitutive irreducibility work to distance further the possible intrusion of negation. The time of the 'at the same time', this moment that is already other than singular, provides the temporality proper to the a part/apart. While the moment may bear a date, and be given a site in the passage of chronology, what it sites and hence sets in place is a timed moment, perhaps even a timed time, that cannot itself be reduced to the time of dating and chronology. Time comes to be incorporated into the work. The work becomes timed. Allowing for the complexity of time (and here complexity means a founding irreducibility) is to allow for the complexity of the object. Time and ontology are necessarily interarticulated in this setup, and it is this interarticulation that opens up the possibility of defining the operation of the becoming-object at the same time as it allows for the insistent presence of the question and therefore of the object-in-question. Accepting the possibilities given by this repositioning of the object will involve a shift in ontological terms. In other words the distinction between the static object, the object that gives and bears its own truth and the becoming-object is a division that can only be accounted for ontologically.

What is the becoming-object? Any attempt to answer this question must start with the recognition that what is being addressed and thus what is being demanded is the being proper to an object being a work of art. While this may seem a cumbersome formulation, and thus one which may complicate unnecessarily considerations that pertain to art, in fact the opposite is the case. It is only by taking up the question of the specificity of the work — what allows or maintains it as it is — that there is a confrontation with what is most pertinent. Asking the question of the object cannot avoid the ontological since what is being demanded (asked for) is the mode of being proper to that object. In other words such questioning is searching to elicit a response to the question of art's being. If the centrality of the ontological is assumed — and here it must be if what is at stake is the existence of the object, its being as art — then the problem of how to approach that centrality automatically arises. How, therefore, is the question of art's being to be approached? While the detail of that question cannot be worked through (and here the detail would mean the examination of the founding philosophical moves in which the question of the art object has been taken up) there are important considerations that nonetheless have already been indicated. Part of what has already been suggested is that one of the defining elements that marks out the presence of an art object is that it retains the question of the object as part of its work. Even though what this may mean in the case of installations and even for certain site-specific sculptures may be clear, it is perhaps less clear when what is at issue is a painting. How is it that the most conventional portrait, for example, maintains the question of the object as a question and with it as an essential part of its work? The answer to this question will necessitate the reintroduction of what might be called the problematic of interpretation. In all these examples — both in terms of what has been cited thus far and the analyses to come — what is central is the object of interpretation and with it the activity of interpretation.

The art object is given within interpretation. What follows from this designation and hence location is that the object is twice positioned; the positioning will always have to involve an inescapable interconnection. In the first case the object is positioned in relation to generic determinations; for example the conditions of possibility that pertain to portraiture will necessarily pre-exist any one portrait. Moreover, part of the generic determination is that on the most minimal level — and here the minimal means the level of purpose and function — the nature of the division between art and non-art is also already established. It should be added of course that even though there is a way of stating and maintaining the division between art and non-art within the terms set by the minimal distinction, it nonetheless remains the case that what is necessarily left unposed within it is the question of the object. In the second case the positioning involves that in terms of which interpretation is possible. Accepting that the act of interpretation can be given a transcendental description allows on the one hand that the material practices of interpretation are always enacted and sustained within their own history, while, on the other hand, it means that questions of dominance can be taken up and countered within interpretation in that dominance which is acted out due to the transcendental hold tradition has on the possibility of interpretation itself.

What, then, is the relationship between interpretation understood as necessarily interconnected with the operation of tradition, and the art object understood as the becoming-object? As the connection with tradition may have either a negative or a positive character — ie tradition's determination will be repeated within the reign of the Same or there will be a disruptive and thus destructive relation — there can be no straightforward and generalisable answer; any answer will depend on the specificity of the work in question. (It should be added here that the problem of generality will be in part diminished in taking up the work of specific works.) However, to the extent that the connection is understood as involving a repetition that takes place beyond the repetition of the Same and hence is one where the connection involves the interplay of abeyance and destruction, then the relationship will be necessarily discordant. A hint has already been given as to why this lack of accord must pertain. In outline, the reason for the lack is that the operation of tradition takes place in terms of a dominant ontologico-temporal setup which is fundamentally different to the one that belongs to the becoming-object. There is a different sense and formation of propriety. It is not as though the operation of history — once that history is thought philosophically — operates outside of ontological and temporal considerations. Indeed both will figure — figuring within their different modalities — in any philosophical conception of historical time. As has already been suggested the movement of interpretation, in that it takes place within the varying forms or permutations of repetition, opens up the possibility of an interpretation that gives the object of interpretation in a way that had not been signalled in advance. If the inaugurating repetition, by breaking with or failing to repeat the Same — the Same being that which is given, the work of tradition, in order to be repeated — opens up such a possibility, then not only does this necessitate taking up the ontology and temporality of interpretation it demands, but at the same time, that the object itself comes to be considered, or perhaps reconsidered. Prompting this consideration would be the recognition that it was the object that sanctioned and occasioned the act of interpretation; specifically, here, that particular interpretive act which released the object — the given object — from its already given place. What is at work in this possibility is more than the act of interpretation if that act is thought to involve little more than the progressive interchange of opinions. It is, rather, the affirmation of the already inscribed formulation of both the object — its implicit ontology and temporality — and the conception of historical time within the process of interpreta-tion. Their presence is productive even if it were thought to be absent. Arguing for their absence is already a stand within ontology, temporality and historical time. Interpretation, in other words, brings these three elements into play and as the object is only ever given within interpretation that play is, once more, of the essence.[7] As will be noted, the presence of this necessity is linked to the opening of a field of activity rather than a delimitation of possibility.

And yet while time and existence figure within this formulation of object and tradition, it could nonetheless always be objected that what is occurring with their use and therefore equally within this attempted formulation of art object amounts to an unnecessary and unwarranted complication. Complications would not be precluded but, within the frame of such an argument, the question of the object would only ever become complicated when the determinations with which it is given are not allowed to pertain. Why should it be necessary to raise the question of the object in this particular way? Is it not possible to address the object as no more than either a cultural or historical entity? The answer to these questions must be unequivocal. The question of the object should be raised in this way since if the question insists then both that which is allowing it to insist and that within which it is insisting pertain to the being in question, to the object being what it is; in sum, to its being art. In other words the question of the object must be raised if an effective study of the object is to be undertaken. Here there is a recourse to the transcendentalism that, in the end, concerns philosophical thinking. Within the recognition of the need to take up the question of the object (again a need compounded by part of the work's work being the taking up of that question, hence the formulation object-in-question) the interconnection of time and existence must also be allowed to pertain. Maintaining the ineliminable presence of the ontologico-temporal will provide the precise point at which it becomes possible to return to the becoming-object. Returning to the object in this sense is once more to hold to the centrality of interpretation while incorporating within it the ineliminable presence of ontology, temporality and history.

What is captured immediately by the formulation becoming-object is the linkage or, perhaps more accurately, the incorporation of the object into a process, one which concerns its coming to presence. From the start therefore it is differentiated from other accounts of the object. Once more any serious account of the basis of this differentiation will have to have recourse both to ontology and temporality since the nature of the difference between conceptions of the object, if it is to be a real difference, must involve the interarticulated presence of ontology and time. Moreover it is the process of presentation that captures what marks out the object as art work. What this means is that the becoming-object is an attempt to reformulate the question of the object that is no longer determined by the traditional formulation of the object. And yet, rather than offering a simple relativity, what is also being suggested is that the becoming-object is a formulation that captures and expresses what is proper to the being of art work. The modality of becoming, linked necessarily to the centrality of giving, is a way of accounting for the life of the object in which what is given can never be coextensive or identical with any one instance of its being given. While this process is intrinsic to the art work, it must always be recognised that the nature of the difference between what amounts to the life and the afterlife of a work needs to be understood in ontological terms. The impossibility, moreover, of excluding the afterlife, the object's capacity to live on — an impossibility which is once again an integral part of the work's being — means that as an object it is continually coming to presence. The object's own history is the history of that *presencing*. Its being as an object is also itself inscribed with this specific construal of the continuity of coming to presence; a continuity that will maintain as ontologically distinct the continuity of becoming and the specificity of a particular presentation. They will be maintained as distinct even though they may be materially connected, if not imbricated, in the work's work. In sum, this interplay of continuity and presentation is the becoming-object.

Within this formulation there are two aspects that are of great significance and which will have to be pursued. Both can be presented as an integral part of a countering move that opens out beyond the language and thinking of simple op-positions. The first involves representation while the second concerns the consequent need both to rethink and reformulate the nature of the distinction between what is presented at a given moment — presented within and as interpretation — and the copresent conditions for future and different interpretive presentations; the work of the becoming-object. In taking up these aspects of the becoming-object it might then be possible to situate the reworking of the object within the terms set by the working of tradition.

## Representation, Repetition, Question

Even in conceding the problem of generality it is still possible to specify the work of representation. It will be the work of an ontologically distinct realm. Accepting this as a point of departure will mean that here representation refers to the possibility that the object will either give or be able to give its own historical or interpretive frame. It is within this frame that the object is to be understood — it becomes an object of understanding — such that the activity of interpretation becomes the re-presentation within the language and the practice of interpretation, interpretation's own self-proclaimed activity, of that singular and necessarily unified determination. Here time and ontology figure in a precise sense. The temporality of the object must be such that when given, when it gives itself to and for interpretation, it is given absolutely. All that is to be given is given. Donation here is measured and established against what is possible. Representation in this sense sets the scene with regard to the possibility of interpretation, the actuality of interpretation and the nature of what it is that is interpreted. All three of these elements are interconnected and establish a limit. What establishes and reinforces this limit is the possibility of another conception of object in which the alterity in question is the relation of non-relation (a formulation demanded by the recognition of the impossibility of complete destruction) that emerges with the becoming-object. If representation, understood as the re-presentation of the singular and unified, is itself that which dominates both the practice of interpretation and the ontological formulation of the object within that practice, then the becoming-object involves a differentiation from the work of dominance and thus from the work of tradition. The most elementary form taken by this distinction is set by the nature of the difference between representation and repetition.

Perhaps the most troubling element of this distinction is that it is a distinction between two different types of repetition. In the case of representation — both the force and the end of representation — is that an identifiable content comes to be given — re-given and thus re-presented — such that what is given within and as interpretation neither adds nor subtracts from what was intended to be given. (Representation incorporates a necessary teleology.) Consequently truth will pertain to the object's subject matter, and it will be this matter that is identified and re-presented.[8] The identification of a singular content entails that what is given cannot affect or alter the re-presentation of that singularity. Thus there is a constitutive aspiration for a simple repetition. It is within the terms set by this aspiration that identifying the apparently aporetic within representation will be contingent upon having accepted representation's possibility in the first place. In addition it would not be just its possibility but the conception of object and history within which it was articulated which would also have had to have been assumed in order that the identification of their impossibility could then be significant. (As will be noted, the abeyance of representation will not entail the eschewing of any attempt to take up presentation.) However, the becoming-object is not the work arising from the impossibility of representation; the object within becoming is not the work of the negative and consequently not the *via negativa*, impossibility's own work. Rather than linking it to the negative what will be involved here is an importantly different sense of alterity. Holding to the productive centrality of the becoming-object, therefore, will mean that it is essential to reiterate the claims made both explicitly and implicitly throughout the preceding. In the first place it will be that it is only in terms of an ontology and temporality of becoming that the force of the art object will be able to be located. Becoming is the ontology proper to the art work since it is only in terms of becoming that it is possible for the work to work. Secondly, it is only in terms of becoming that there can be an adequate account of the possibility of conflicting interpretations both at the present and then through time (the latter being chronology's time). If representation is to be understood as a form of repetition — a form already distanced by the truth of art work, namely the becoming-object — how, then, is what presents itself to be understood? What is it that is given within interpretation? With these questions it is vital to return to work, to the object's work. Furthermore it will be with this return that it will then become possible to take up the specificity of work. Part of the analysis of the object's particularity will be the logic of the apart/a part. Now, however, the logic's own work will have been situated with and thus as part of the becoming-object. Tracing the movement of this logic will occur in the specific discussions to come.

Work has taken on the quality of a process of enactment. And yet as the enacting is the specificity and the particularity of the work's presentation — its own self-presentation as (its) work — that presentation has to be given a positive description. What is present is what occurs. The occurrence understood as the work is the work's material presence. While this location of matter is accurate, what will emerge both in its generality and in the treatment of Boltanski and Langlands & Bell in particular, is that even though materiality functions as the work's base, the work's work cannot be made coextensive with its material presence. Allowing for irreducibility is, once more, the inevitable consequence of the way the work functions. With the becoming-object the materiality is incorporated into the process of interpretation. However it is also more than incorporation as what takes place with interpretation is the move that allows for the question of the art object to be given and thus to have a general presence at the same time as it has a particular formulation. The particularity in question is not an additional part of the object; it forms an essential part of its work. Part of the force of the *Truisms* is provided by their complex relation to art and to advertising; and the reason for this complexity is provided by the logic of the a part/apart. Here what this will mean is that their presence as art does not obviate the need to take up the question of their presence as art. In order that they function and thus have the effect that they have, part of their work must be to allow that question — art's question    to remain unresolved. Allowing it to remain in that state will mean that the particularity of art and non-art is held up and examined from within the context of art work. Rather than pursuing the consequences and effects of specific works, what is of interest here is the way in which the object works. Work stands in contradistinction to the positing of an object and the subsequent attribution of qualities to it. With the question being maintained the object has become the object in-question. There is, however, an obvious objection.

The objection is simply that, even though this may be an adequate description of Jenny Holzer's *Truisms*, why and on what basis could it be generalised to incorporate the art object itself? Responding must take place with the recognition that a minimal distinction between art and non art is already in place; it is already given. As has been suggested, however, in its traditional formulation the question of the object is excluded from playing a role in the distinction's formulation. What happens once that latter question — the question of the object — comes to be included is that the precise determination of the object is never complete. Part of what allows for this irreducible infinite as opposed to the finitude of completion is the temporality of the question. The question is held as a question. It is of course not held as the site of a semantic and interpretive postponement or deferral; on the contrary, it is part of the work's work and therefore belongs to the object itself. Irreducibility figures with the question. The becoming-object works in connection with the object-in-question to the extent that the irreducibility of the former means that the way in which the object functions as art will always be present as a question. Its presence is not as an abstract question that is added on to the object; rather, the insistent question must always be allowed a regional and precise presence and a determining role in the presence of the work's work.

# Matter and Meaning: On Installations and Sites

**H**aving allowed the problem of the object to emerge, and having allowed that emergence to be positioned in relation to the object understood in terms of what has been identified thus far as the becoming-object; then having positioned the work of that object as necessarily present with, and therefore as inextricably linked to, the object-in-question, it is now possible to rework the place of the object in terms of two specific possibilities or practical undertakings within the visual arts. The first is the installation and the second is what has been designated as 'site-specific' sculpture. (In this instance what is of central interest is the nature of what is designated as the 'site' rather than the presence of sculpture as such.) It will be seen, however, that while maintaining the specificity of each there are important moments of interconnection. Tracing both their specificity as well as their connections will allow the dynamic quality of the object to be elaborated further. In concentrating on movement, work and time, what has been identified in general as the actative and what will arise is the possibility of giving a redescription of the site's formation. Matter will emerge as grounding that which will always be more than the merely material; in other words what matters will constitute another form and thus another take on material presence. Matter will have been integrated with time and therefore, in the recognition of that setup, its already present temporalisation will come to be affirmed. Matter will come to the site of the move from occurrence to event.[1]

## Installations

Taking up the installation involves locating it within what has been developed thus far in terms of the continual attempt by art's own activity, its work — an activity that can only ever be adequately traced by the retroactive and constitutive process of critique and interpretation — to bring the question of the specificity of the object into play. Art will turn around that question by repeating its own formation as question. A consequence of this location, this turning questioning, involves accepting the premise that the installation's meaning is, in part, structured by its own particular negotiation with the question of the object. With such a negotiation — a negotiation here to be understood as eschewing a teleological frame and thus maintaining itself as a negotiation without end — art, and its formal presentation in terms of the object, is continually present as a question. As will be suggested the installation's work — its effective presence — is sanctioned, hence its own activity is repeated, by that question remaining open; its work will take that opening as its site. It will be held as open even in the continuity of its being addressed. The installation in both its particularity as well as its generality can be described as taking its place and thus as being at work within that opening. Maintaining the presence of this opening, maintaining it not as an addition but as constitutive of work, holds in place that which gives the installation its own specific critical dimension. This dimension is itself only possible, and therefore in a more directly philosophical sense only thinkable, because of the ineliminable presence of the object-in-question.

A start can be made by working with the already present recognition that one of the questions around which art continues to turn concerns what it is that gives to the work its specific quality as art. In other words the question that must be addressed is: what is it that allows a given material object to exist as a work of art? It goes without saying that the art market, fashion and the continual slide from art work to commodity form a fundamental part of any answer to such a question. And yet there remains something unsatisfactory about their inclusion in any response if, as a consequence, it is thought to be the complete answer to the question. In general terms art has, of course, continually addressed, and had addressed for it, the question of what it is. Moreover the specific forms within art — painting, sculpture, etc — have been subject to the same attempt to secure and establish their own boundaries. The attempt within the Kantian and therefore modernist tradition to differentiate 'fine art', or more simply the 'beautiful', from mere representation, even from a mimetic presentation of 'fine art' or the 'beautiful', has come to figure as the attempt to establish that which was unique about the work of art. An attempt that leads inexorably to the formulation of different conceptions of autonomy all of which play a determining role in the constitution of different construals of modernity.[2] Not only painting but sculpture and the other 'fine arts' were included in the attempt to maintain a justified differentiation of art from non-art. It should not be thought, however, that this distinction remains secure. Indeed, it is possible to argue that its traditional determinations have become increasingly less stable; and working with the slip of stability even helps to mark out that which figures as the contemporary in practices of the visual arts. However, the contemporary will always have to mark out more than what is given by the actual presence of times and dates.

Even though instability characterises oppositional thinking, it should not be too rapidly generalised since it is usually established either as the consequence of a specific interpretation or by the advent of new art practices. In the case of the former what this means is that the traditional formulation of the distinction 'art/non-art', comes undone by showing (showing as an interpretive act) the fragility and, in the end, the impossibility of maintaining the distinction as absolute and thus as all-inclusive. In the latter it is that the advent of film and more recently video, for example, has had the effect of mediating, and in the end frustrating, any attempt to secure the distinction as it is traditionally envisaged. Both of these presentations are such that their very nature makes it difficult to incorporate them in a straightforward and unproblematic way on either side of the art/non-art divide. As a result, therefore, that which holds up the division is brought into question. Furthermore, and as has already been indicated, what is necessitated by this setup is that, at the very least, there is a reformulation of the relationship between art and its other in terms of both the becoming-object of the art work, and therefore allowing for the art object's continual presence as the effective continuity of the object-in-question. Becoming, once again, moves in (and into) the place of static being.

There is therefore a further possibility; what in the end will have amounted to a different adventure within, and for, the visual arts. As an opening what must be taken up — though here it will be a retaking introducing different determinations — is another response to the question of why the distinction between art and its other will always be marked by a potential instability. The initial answer will be that the reason for this instability is art's inherent materiality. Its material and physical presence announces that despite everything else the work of art is an object, a material object. Nonetheless, in taking up the work of art, its materiality is often effaced in favour of the consequence of art's material presence. Emphasising, for example, the way in which the work of sculpture creates space necessitates the absorption of the materiality such that it — the materiality — is repositioned as the support of spacing. Materiality works here by its buttressing the object's art work. If, in contradistinction to the effacing of material presence, it is made immediately central, then the question of what counts as a work immediately opens up. The repositioning of matter and therefore of the materiality of the art object is not to be taken as simple empiricism; what would amount to the uncritical positing of objects. While matter is central, it is matter's work — the activity that it sanctions — that will indicate however that, on its own, matter is not sufficient. Matter is not there as an end in itself. It is never just on its own. With matter what will also have to be introduced is the impossibility of positing materiality as present — and therefore as having a specific presence — outside of the operation of signification. Matter is thereby given with meaning. Meaning is the gift that is based on the event. As has already been sketched, the recognition of the event and thus the recognition of interpretation as moving from occurrence to event is ineliminably linked to the process of affirmation.

One way of taking the interplay of matter, meaning and the objectivity of art leads inexorably to the problem of ornamentation, whilst another way leads to a specific type of questioning that finds its most insistent source in Duchamp and the 'ready-made'. It is the latter that will be of concern here; a concern which while not conflating the ready-made with the installation assumes, nonetheless, that the installation derives, in part, its conditions of existence from the former. It is not necessary here to rehearse the complex impact of the ready-made (an impact that opened up different and, in the end, incompatible possibilities within art practices). All that needs to be indicated, at this stage, is that with the ready-made the problem of objectivity and the question of what is to count as a work of art — the art object — is itself intensified. An object that already existed and hence which was *already* located outside of the sphere of art — the sphere minimally constructed by the interrelated presence of exhibition and criticism/interpretation — is incorporated into that sphere by its being exhibited, in a sense its being renamed, and with that incorporation is then located within the margins of art practice.[3] The problem to be faced is, in the first place, accounting for how it is that what was initially excluded from the domain of art has, in an as yet to be defined movement, come to be included within it. In the second place, what must then be given is a philosophical rather than either a sociological or historical account of the process of exclusion and inclusion. Starting by working from the other direction, what can be asked for, at least initially, is a move that in the first place takes up the question of how the exclusion could be maintained — what sustains the place of art's other — and then in the second place, why it should have been necessary for it to have been maintained at all. The questioning of art's other is thus a move made in a more general displacing of any simple formulation of the distinction between art and non-art. The work of oppositions — of what opposes — cannot itself be posited.

It is tempting, in working within the terms set by these questions, to argue that a given object should not have been included within the domain of art objects because of the precise nature of its — the object-in-question — materiality. However this on its own is far from adequate, since what must be added is that an essential part of its non-inclusion would be that it was already located within a defined set of established meanings. In other words, integral to any argument for a specific object not being art is that its meaning — in terms of its being a specific object — is itself already fixed and established. It would have had a meaning therefore that by definition (and here the force of the definition would have to be marked by a certain necessity) fell outside the purview of art (art's own meaning). Materiality therefore, as has been suggested, is from the start positioned within an already present structure of meaning. Recognising the ineliminable reciprocity between meaning and matter will overcome the interpretive and philosophical naivety occasioned by the simple positing of objects. Consequently with this present position there are three different points which, in being made, allow for the inherent complexity of this reworking of the relationship between art and its other in terms of the interplay to be taken up of matter and meaning. These three points will sanction strategic interconnections; and tracing these relationships will allow not just the place of the installation to be opened up but its being held open by the constitutive role within it of the object-in-question. Again the continuity in question is the placed movement of the becoming-object; the object's work. It will be the terms set by this complex opening up that will allow a connection to be drawn with the 'site-specific'. In both instances specificity, while being central will, nonetheless, always be mediated by the nature of the object and thus the way it is present.

The first point arising from the already present connection of matter and material is that, while the material presence of the art object — the frame and the canvas, for example — works to locate the painting within the sphere of art, the work of that material presence also precludes its immediate absorption into another domain of meaning. What this entails with this example is that it is painting's materiality that works to hold it in place. This gives rise to the second point: what makes the ready-made important for any consideration, or reconsideration, of the nature of the art object is that it indicates that this restriction does not work, in any straightforward way, when the reverse situation pertains.

What this will involve is that the ready-made — the object forming that which is redescribed as 'ready-made' — will be admitted, and admitted unproblematically to the domain of art irrespective of the quality and specificity of its materiality. Initially the object-in-question is only allocated a place by virtue of its materiality. What emerges retrospectively is that its material presence is neither completely held nor absolutely determined by the structure of meaning in which it was initially articulated. There is thus an important distinction to be drawn here between two types of determination, namely the distinction between the determination of matter within the sphere of art as opposed to the determination outside of it. What the ready-made creates, however, is another take on these determinations. As part of the movement between domains, the consequence is that the materiality of the object will have overcome its location and meaning outside of the sphere of art. In part this is because matter, while presented in terms of function, does not lose its materiality once the given function no longer pertains.

The ready-made, therefore, could almost be taken as being the supreme articulation of art without utility; in other words in necessarily resisting function it emerges as paradigmatically without purpose. And yet of course this may well be the limit of the ready-made. In fact it is possible to go further by arguing that while the ready-made opened up the possibility of the installation by making problematic the question of the art object in its differentiation from the non-art object, it occupied an ambivalent position. The ambivalence emerges because what is involved here is a straightforward repetition, albeit in another form, of the classical determination of art as having no purpose outside of itself. Here the variant is that the object sustains its own irreducibility to function while presenting, even if in a form that is itself non-functional, that which has (or had) a function. Both of these elements must occur at the same time. It is thus that what allows the ready-made to work is the logic of the apart/a part. Here the role of that logic not only gives the ready-made; it also works to allow for another formulation of the art/non-art distinction by indicating the place of a constitutive parasitism. The complex repetition that rids the object of its coextensivity with function works to the extent that the repeated object bears a relation to the functionality that no longer pertains as such. What the ready-made opens up, therefore, is an-other possibility for matter. The ambivalence that marks the material presence of the ready-made creates an opening that is founded in matter; moreover it will be in terms of that opening that it will become possible to locate the site and thus the specificity of the installation's work. Again, the logic of the apart/a part in providing the art object maintains it and allows it to work — where work will always involve a necessary and strategic specificity — by holding open as a question the nature of the object. This is, of course, the effective presence of the object as object-in-question. (The detail and with it the regional force of this formulation will emerge in the following consideration of the work of Langlands & Bell and Christian Boltanski.)

The final point that arises here, and which can also be linked to the above considerations, concerns sculpture. Once matter is taken into consideration then the relation between art and non-art will be at its most complex in relation to sculpture. Part of the complexity involves the relationship that material presence has to both ornament and function. A constituent element of sculpture's role was to ornamentalise; and, in being an ornament, its function was in part reduced to its being-as-ornament. Sculpture, therefore, as either monument or symbol, was defined by this expression of its specific being. This definitional hold on sculpture, however, is freed with abstraction — opened up in the process of abstraction. Yet the freedom in question is delimited by function. It is checked by it and consequently its work is held by the relationship between matter and function; the latter will, of course, always allow for its own negative presence. What this means is that to the extent that abstraction held itself apart from function, what was presented was assumed to be the simple materiality of the sculptural; in sum, its material form. With abstraction, therefore, sculpture is taken up with the possibility of its being the enactment of the purity and the simplicity of form. (A path is opened up here to minimalism within sculpture.) Without here attempting to investigate the viability of this possibility, what must be noted is that the freedom of abstraction occurring in the process of abstracting — albeit what in the end will turn out to have been an illusory freedom — in enacting the arbitrary hold of function and ornament, opens up as a question that will, henceforth, control and delimit material presence. With sculpture, therefore, the arbitrary will be introduced; and what will count as sculpture will incorporate the arbitrary for two reasons. The first reason is that the arbitrary stems from the indeterminacy of signification resulting from the break up of the tight relation between sculpture, function and ornament; and, secondly, it arises because of sculpture's materiality. It is clear that these reasons are connected. The result is that the materiality of sculpture will potentially allow for any material form to be presented as sculpture. Matter's presence will no longer be fixed as the primary site of signification. Of the many possibilities this founding lack of fixity will allow, one of the most insistent will be the installation. Installations however will, in the nature and divergence of their work, no longer be held by the problems posed by a simple materiality, and yet the lack of fixity will in a more general sense allow them to work as art works. They will work with these problems in opening up other adventures and activities for art's practice.

The departure that sets up and identifies the practice of the installation will also be linked to the ready-made. With the ready-made what occurs is that the interruption of the signifying system in which the object was initially located disrupts the space in which it will come to be placed. Originally the material presence of the object entailed that its meaning was never such that the matter and meaning could ever have been coextensive even if they were both delimited by function. (Again it is the effective presence of an original plurality. In this instance, however, its presence only emerges retrospectively.) The relocation of the object, its transformation into a work of art, derives its conditions of existence from that founding lack of coextensivity — a lack stemming from matter and which will itself always be in excess of simple functionality — and reproduces the impossibility of that closure in its transformation into an object. The ready-made carries and displays its original function but displaces it, since it always opens itself beyond the effectivity given by that function. Consequently, in no longer being reducible to that which is enacted by and as function, the object, which is now the ready-made, allows for space by incorporating a productive spacing. The spacing arises precisely because the material repetition (materially the object is the same) is that which allows for the repetition in which what is repeated is *not* the same. The presence of this constitutive spacing in holding the object-in-question in place, in giving by constituting that object, generates that which is beyond the sway of prediction and works within and with the effective abeyance of teleology. It is this spacing that was originally given with the first relation between matter and meaning and which, after the event, gets reinscribed in (and into) the object's transformation (again, the logic of the apart/a part). In the latter case the spacing allows matter to be the work of art, the object, and in being it to do art's work. It will be a work, however, that in falling beyond the hold of symbol, ornament and function eschews, at the same time, the hold of prediction. The work in question will incorporate the art of installation by resisting its essentiality. Installations, therefore, will work within the complex space opened up by these differing determinations. Working with, while at the same time holding in place, the object-in-question.

In sum, what allows installations to have their effect in the first place is their founding position given by their relation to both sculpture and the ready-made. It is a relation that is itself only made possible and given the space to work — thus also for work — because of matter, and with matter its necessary interarticulation with meaning. Art's material presence, present here with the installation, founds and confounds sites of signification and in so doing allows for a practice that, in the continuity of the creation of a topos and thereby in the resisting of restrictions, constitutes an opening for meaning. This continuity is the work of art; its being at work in the continuity is once again the affirmation of the reworking of the object in terms of the becoming-object. It will be possible to develop this point by linking it to what is often described as *site-specific* work (an activity that links and conflates installations and sculpture but whose actual specificity remains to be fixed). With this work another important connection and point of disruption can be drawn between installations and sculpture. As always, the point in question necessarily involves the question of the object; the object existing in its state of being as a question.

## Site-Specific

The work proper to installations and sculpture can be linked in that both are able to maintain an essential relation to their site; their specific location. However, while this elementary formulation contains a certain degree of accuracy, its presentation of the founding relations of the site-specific is neither accurate nor adequately complex. Allowing for that complexity will mean that in working through these relations, the specific nature of the designation 'site-specific' will itself have to be questioned. What will emerge is that it will have to be more — and therefore it will always have to have been more — than the simple posited recognition of the pervasive and necessary presence of a given geography. The positing of place leaves the question of the site unposed. The initial difficulty with this undertaking hinges on how the link — the link between work and site — is to be understood. Nonetheless, suggesting that despite the absence of detail the link is central, will work to bring to the fore a specific form of questioning. With any link, and therefore within any relation, the constitutive elements are traditionally thought to have been given and, consequently, given with their own unique determinations. This presumption has to be challenged from the start; and undertaking such a task — the sustained challenging of tradition — is best begun by questioning the possibility of any form of neutrality. The point of such an opening is straightforward since with the display of most art works, be they works paintings or sculptures located within an institutional space (for example a museum or gallery, display is often taken to involve either an assumed or an enforced neutrality. The neutrality exists to the extent that the site is not allowed any form of determining role in the production of the work's meaning; in other words that the site is not taken as forming an essential and constitutive part of the work's work. Even accepting this restriction a distinction does, however, still need to be made at this point; a distinction between, on the one hand, that setup in which the site forms an important but contingent part of the work's understanding or interpretation and, on the other hand, the repositioned site in which the site is taken as forming part of the work itself. With this second possibility — site as intrinsic to the becoming-object — what will come to be demanded is a reconsideration of the nature of what it is that comprises the work. In this latter case the identification of the object — the specific material presence of the object — will itself already have been made problematic, if only because the site can no longer just function as an adjunct or a supplement. It will be in terms of this overall distinction that it will be possible to continue the questioning of neutrality while at the same time opening up the complexity inherent in the link between the work and its site; even its specific and singular site.

Even though the distinction between 'site as contingent' and 'site as already part of the work's work' incorporates a necessary fragility, it must nonetheless still be pursued. At work within it are those determinations that pertain to art's display. Within that display there is an ineliminable and thus primordial doubling; ie a doubling that is already present. While this presence can be either overlooked or forgotten it remains the case that, with any display, what will always be able to insist as a question is: what is it that the display displays? The reason for referring to this setup as the doubling of display is that it allows, in the first place, that doubling to form an integral part of the work's work while, in the second, it opens up that other display as more than a simple addition. If the other dimension were only thought to be an addition — a contingent adjunct — then it would remain as secondary to any consideration of work. As an addition, in other words, it would only be thought to relate to the exhibition of works and thus not to the works themselves. In sum, the doubling would not have been taken as an essential part of the work's being.

However, the contrary is the case since it is the effective presence of this doubling that works to undermine the positing of an unproblematic neutrality. Because of its clear importance — its turning the question of the object away from its traditional determinations — it is this point that needs to be developed. It must be recognised of course that the importance and the role attributed to the doubling of display will always involve pragmatic and thus regional considerations; it will therefore be more appropriate with certain genres and practices than with others. In addition doubling's own inherent complexity pertains to the extent to which this presence — an anoriginal doubled presence — works both within the frame, in the case of painting, and in a broader sense to the presentation of the object where the boundary between object and non-object is not itself firmly fixed, and thus the doubling pertains to the object's presence as such. (The lack of fixity works both by forming and informing the work.) Its role in relation to the internality of the work will always be mediated by the more problematic question of boundary and object. In the end the interplay of boundary and object will be reincorporated as it will always have been part of the work's work. It may therefore be that neither boundary nor object is given; rather, they form a constitutive part of the work's own activity. Pursuing this possibility would involve stripping the interplay's components of whatever neutrality they were ever thought to have had.

The distinction that belongs to the formulation of the site when taken in addition to the varying possibilities at work within display, indicate the inherent complexity at work within the site and therefore within the attempt to make the site specific. These possibilities harbour the complexity and with it the importance of what is marked out — albeit provisionally since all such markings (what in the end is a form of naming) express pragmatic concerns — as the site specific. While the trap inherent within any distinction is its instability — the point at which the work done by distinctions will, in its being done, come to be undone — the importance of maintaining a division here should not be played down. What the division indicates is that there are at least two different types of work at play. In the first place there is the work that takes location or site as central. Locating it — thereby relocating it — is the active work of critique or interpretation (a move signalling the primordial and effective presence of time since it is time which allows them — critique, interpretation — to figure).

In the second place there is a more ambiguous relation between the object and its location. In this instance the site forms part of the object. And yet the difficulty here is establishing the exact way these determinations work. Again the way ahead must be to trace a way through the less difficult case. In that particular instance what is at stake is the location of an object of interpretation in a particular setting in which the interplay between all the formal components of the setting themselves may work to form part of the overall interpretation. Here, by contrast, the relation will be contingent. It pertains, for example, to the relationship between a particular object and its institutional setting. The importance attributed to museums and their determining effect on the display of art objects can be located at this point. There is no need to think however that the relation is necessary or that it necessarily relates to the internal workings of what has been framed; ie the internal specificity of the object. Nor moreover can this type of relation be taken as exhaustive, it is simply one possible domain of interpretation. The question that endures within such an interpretive move, however, is whether or not it takes the art object as the object of interpretation. There will always be the risk that what is being interpreted is a setting that, once taken within the ambit of the interpretive act, precludes the possibility of attention being given to the work's work. Consequently in this particular case what in general terms is involved is the use of location or site to establish — though to establish contingently — an interpretive setting for the object. Nonetheless, while the attribution of this role to a given setting is a real possibility, neither the site nor the setting is going to play a necessary and determining role in what it is that is displayed by the internal work of the object. Internality here will be descriptive of the space delimited, again provisionally, by the frame (the frame as both the interpretive as well as the material site of the object).

While it will be necessary to retain the specificity of what is present within the frame — retaining it even while allowing it to be reworked, perhaps therefore reframed — something else is at play. The contingency of the setting and thus the important though arbitrary role of a given site is limited, since what cannot be addressed let alone engendered by it is the possibility that the site may play a different type of determining role. The determination in question, however, will no longer be either semantic, or simply interpretive or pragmatic, but will relate to what the object is taken to be. This repositioning of the object should not be conflated with the simple positing of an object. Indeed the contrary is the case, for here, rather than taking the object as merely given, it refers to the object as that which *is* in its being given within interpretation; in other words simple existence gives way to the interpretive construal of the object. Part of this process will necessarily involve working from the recognition that if the site is allowed to play a determining role in the constitution of the object, then the boundary between site and object can no longer be taken as fixed. Moreover what will also arise is the necessity to recognise further that this lack of fixity has, in the first place, become part of the work's work and, in the second place, that in each specific instance the nature of that work will incorporate and sustain this precise lack. The lack in question is not the *via negativa* — the melancholic celebration of impossibility that does no more than inaugurate the work of the negative — it is, rather, the affirmed presence of the object as object-in-question. The becoming-object will have supplanted the place of both the given and the posited and as a result of that move, occurring within the move itself, the ontology of the art object will have been reworked. The object will have taken on what has been designated thus far as an-other possibility.

It is at this precise point that the potential within the designation 'site-specific' emerges. While it has a generic determination understood most straightforwardly as the location of a particular art work in a setting in which the setting plays a role in the structuration of the work, it can nonetheless still be given greater force. What is being allowed for here is the real possibility that the determining role of the site may be such that — in its specificity and therefore in its individual and unique determinations — the distinction between site and work comes undone, and in that movement the simple material presence of a given object will no longer be sufficient to answer the question of what it is that the object is. The consequence of this lack is not the impossible but rather that what would emerge in its place, supplanting impossibility, is a different conception of work. The work in question would be one where the attempt to forge a clear and sustained distinction between site and object would have foundered since both would have been taken in their purely material sense. Once more the result of this development — the coming to presence of the becoming-object — will be the reworking of the nature of the object in terms of the interplay between material presence and the site that gives the object. As has already been suggested what that will mean is that what is retained, as a constitutive and therefore productive force, is the question of the object.

Installations and the site-specific involve, therefore, a different take on the question of the object and thus of the object-in-question than that which is assumed to be already at work within the frame. (Of course the latter needs to be taken in the sense that brings both the interpretive and the material into play.) While the framed site presents the material presence of the object and thus leaves, for the most part, the terrain of the becoming object to the actual work of the framed, here the distinction, though in fact the effective continuity of the distinction, between boundary and object in being questioned takes that questioning as an integral part of the work's work. The inability to specify immediately the presence of the object and therefore to be able, again immediately, to differentiate object and content (or object and site) attests to the effective presence of a different setup. Furthermore, it will be in terms of that difference that the work of installations and the 'site-specific' becomes possible. By drawing on that from which they are a part, by holding to a specific place but in redefining the place and thus what is meant by being in it but apart from it, installations and the 'site-specific' are given other determinations with which to work. They operate in terms of the logic of the a part/apart where what determines the place of each as an internality and externality is brought into question and displaced. Placing and displacing, in working together at the same time, reinforce the complexity — the anoriginal complexity — of the work's work. It is this form of complexity that will be traced in terms of their different presentation in the work of Langlands & Bell and Christian Boltanski.

# Material Events: Langlands & Bell

With the work of Langlands & Bell there is always an occasion.[1] At the beginning this occasion is an occurrence; occurring at the place where the work can be said to be taking place and therefore where, initially, it will define a site. This initial formulation in which a site is defined rather than given, opens what is all too often the automatic conflation of object and work; a conflation that automatically positions the site as external to the object. The presence of the site — and when taking the architectural models and the 'furniture' into consideration, what will amount to the sited site — is not in question. The questions that will be seen to unfold within this work are different. They will pertain to what it is that makes the site work as a site. In sum what emerges is the question of what the site sites; what is it that is sited there? In allowing these questions to arise and in their being maintained as questions, the consequence of this difference — perhaps what sanctions their difference — is that the answers traditionally envisaged for any questioning of site and object are no longer apposite; and yet there is a site and there are objects.

Arising with this questioning will be the recognition that both the status of the object and the nature of the site — their own pregiven determinations — are themselves brought into question by virtue of this opening. While the strategies giving rise to this state of affairs remain to be shown, they will have the consequence that what had hitherto been the automatic positioning of site and object no longer works. As such what is demanded — and it is this point that must be allowed to unfold rather than be simply posited — is a reconsideration of the object; a reconsideration which if it is to take up the essential must involve the ontology of the art object itself. In other words the already inaugurated overall project of reworking the object will be allowed to continue. Here the process of generalisation and abstraction must yield their place and thus their interpretive centrality to another and different setup. It is not simply that there must be a concentration on specific works, the concentration must itself work with the recognition that an interpretive language in which these objects are to be judged is yet to be formulated with any sustained precision. Once more the questions will not touch on generality as such. On the contrary, it will be here that the specificity of the object-in-question must be taken up (indeed it will come to insist because of its productive presence) and its work will have to form the locus of discussion. There is a need, therefore, for an opening that will occasion the precision that the work demands; the work in question, the interpretive work that is demanded by the work of Langlands & Bell. Without necessarily being named as such, what follows concerns the specificity of the work.

*Langlands & Bell, Interlocking Chairs, 1989, beech, glass, AC lacquer, 95x102x62cm (reproduced courtesy of Glenn Scott Wright, Contemporary Art)*

## Model Work

In a room there is an elegant table; elegant in its simplicity, if not in its austerity. Elsewhere there is a set of chairs. On walls hang framed architectural models. As a start this is semblance, mere appearance. There is, however, more going on here than can be accounted for in terms of the simple presentation of tables and chairs. And yet despite the presence of this addition, the attribution of a further quality, the force of these occurrences — material enactments — does not lie elsewhere as though what is taking place, the putative real presence, took place behind the appearance, thereby turning presentation into a facade or mask. Here it will be suggested that what occurs, the appearances — the objects — work to undo the logic articulated within, thus at the same time articulating the opposition between appearance and reality. Presentation as veil, semblance as facade, are construals of the object and thus constructions of what is occurring that, once again, are no longer appropriate. The objects are, of course, no less real. The reality of the object — a reality necessarily incorporating materiality — is maintained because this lack of propriety, the lack of what is taken traditionally to be appropriate, is generated by the works in question. If the reality and the materiality of what is taking place — the occurrence being presented, are not to be found behind the appearance and therefore taken as being at work at a depth within it — another beginning will have already been made necessary. Since these works eschew a simple dipping into depths, one yielding the purported overcoming of appearance, they make additional demands on interpretation. The nature of this addition is of singular importance. As an opening what is being distanced — held in abeyance initially with a degree of hesitancy, though in the end with a certain finality — is that construal of the art object in which its truth content is taken as being there, though only at a depth within the object. What happens when the truth and reality of the object is thought to be located at a depth within it is that an intrinsic part of the object is systematically left unquestioned. As a direct consequence what remains unquestioned, except as that which brings the object's truth at a depth within it, is the object's own material presence. Material presence is effaced within the interpretive process in which the only position attributed to that presence is as the material presentation of some other quality. The alterity in question will always be other than material; it will have a different form of presence. There is a related point of equal significance that also needs to be made at this stage. What is also precluded by this move is the possibility that it may be the material which, rather than housing the work, is itself at work. The effacing of material presence is the consequence of opting for matter as that which houses a putative real presence.

Allowing for the centrality of matter — and thus working with the distancing of the proposition that art allows the presencing of the essential — means that here something must be given, something must have occurred. As a way in, therefore, it is possible to start with a question. In this instance, because the question that immediately arises concerns the nature of the object, the question must be: what is a material object? The question is precise. Its precision lies in the already given nature of the object. In other words there already is an object. It is there. What is given, however, has a double determination. In the first place it is present as an object — as an occurrence — and in the second it is given within interpretation. Indeed it is in terms of this second determination — and an object of interpretation — that it is possible to sustain the interpretation of those objects as themselves comprising the *already given*.[2] It will be argued here that what can provisionally be described as a doubling of the given, while dependent upon the material presence of the given, opens up possibilities that are not reducible to what is given materially. There is greater complexity at work here than would be encapsulated in the claim that it is simply the matter — the material presence — which is doubled. And yet the centrality of the material will endure. Indeed, it is only emphasising the object's actual materiality that forces an opening up of elements that are never simply just material. These elements come to be opened up as part of the material object's own constitutive presence and thus as an ineliminable part of its work. (The doubling of matter and with matter's move beyond itself is a further distancing of that conception of the art object that oscillates between the presencing of the essential and the positing of real presence.) This opening needs to be understood as the work of materiality. It is in part what constructs the material occurrence — what is taking place — as that occurrence. The opening is sustained, however, in the move from occurrence to event. (It will be essential to return both to the directionality and with it to the temporality of this move.) Matter's situation is ineliminably linked to meaning (the latter incorporating the activity of interpretation, ie the attribution of meaning) and therefore material presence cannot be approached except in relation to the possibility of its being attributed meaning.

Before taking up the specificity of the chair or table, and in relation to such works their specificity means the detail of what occurred, it is vital to stay with the object itself, the initial and thus insistent occurrence. The point here is that the opening, the object occasioning something other than what has already been given as the occurrence, while demanding a material base — the opening must stem from the material presence of the object — its work cannot be reduced to that which is given with (also as) the object's occurrence. What will come to be the object's work will itself be based on a reworking of the occurrence. (In more general philosophical terms what this means is that the occurrence will emerge, retrospectively, as being conditioned by the event.[3]) To be specific it is necessary to argue that the force of both the table and chair is not found in what is presented. In other words it does not lie in the simple presentation of the interplay of material presence and function. Here, with these works, the presence of function will always be more complex. Now, and even though it would still the force of this complexity, it could, nonetheless, be argued in relation to these objects that part of their work would demand that the function of the chair or table is employed, and then, after that, it is deployed beyond its function. From within one construal of this movement, that additional move, marked out here by the 'and then', would signal the presence of a developmental shift. From a single origin the chair or table as functional would be allowed a second life in which function was no longer central. Within the framework of this argument there would be the presupposition of a straightforward move from the simple to the complex. Despite its initial appeal, the flaw within this entire developmental setup is not in the move itself but rather is there in the presupposition of a founding and original singularity. The development indicated by the 'and then' must be resisted because neither the chair nor the table were ever just functional. There was never a founding simplicity — an original singularity — even though functionality will continue to endure as a fundamental component of the object's being. Therefore, while being tables and chairs they were never *just* tables and chairs. The important point here is that both these designations occur at the same time. It will be this time that is central since what it will bring with it is the temporality of complexity; a temporality whose presence gestures towards the inescapable necessity of the occurrence's founding complexity. Here this gesture repositions the occurrence by showing that it maintains the effective presence of the event.

What is being given a place within the opening allowed by the complex origin, is a space in which the object is repeated. Repetition will demand its own temporality. Indeed the repetition in question will involve what has already been identified as the logic of the a part/ apart. This gives rise to that copresence in which what occurs while taking place again is also, and at the same time, taking place anew. The recognition of this twofold presence, as that which is presented at the same time, is the retroactive constitution of the occurrence as event. It is thus that this copresence is never just a simple presence — not simple because the origin is from the start constructed by an irreducible complexity; it is anoriginally irreducible. The irreducibility does not involve a relation between two occurrences; rather, the split, the irreducibility, the founding complexity, the spacing, are all constitutive of the event as an anoriginally heterogeneous event and therefore each will form an essential part of the work's work. Here the event is brought to the fore by this other repetition. Consequently it is the copresence — the presence, at the same time, of the determination as function and the yet to be determined — which will necessitate further consideration. What is taking place with these occurrences, these objects, must be understood as the productive presence of the logic of the apart/a part; moreover, the works in question will demand that the relation between the simultaneous though different determinations be pursued. Due to the role played by time, part of this further consideration will be taking up the interplay of ontology and time within the complex object. Part of this activity will be the attempt to trace how the interplay between them sustains the object as complex and therefore as *a* complex.

The chairs, the tables and the architectural models attract attention, holding the viewers gaze in part because of an already established self-sustaining (and of course self-made) claim about their identity. Their identity is already given; moreover the representational quality of the models often allows their referents to be identified immediately. (The interpretive difficulties posed by the aesthetic quality will be taken up at a later stage.) Architectural models, tables and chairs are already present; traditionally they are already in place. In being in place they bring their own pregiven determinations with them. They are already a part of a given set; a pregiven interrelation of matter and meaning. What comes to be announced, therefore, is their presence as table, chair or model (a presence that brings both function and utility with it). While this presence is mediated by their exhibition, what nonetheless cannot be escaped is their material presence. However, as has already been suggested, contemporaneous with this presence is the impossibility of the complete reduction to function.

Function's presence within their work — within its work — has an important and insistent presence. Langlands & Bell are already aware that function enjoins a certain response. Its presence sets certain demands in play that cannot be avoided:

> What is important to us is how its [a building's] function is represented, how pervasively the design of the structure is informed by the final purpose of the building.[4]

There is more at work here than the representation of function, for what their work aims at is the presentation of a representation; it incorporates a complex doubling or repetition. In other words the architectural model, for example, is not just the model of a building; nor, moreover, is it in a strict sense an architectural model. Whilst being a model it is more. And in being more it is not just that it is always already more, but that it indicates that the model — the actual architectural model — will itself already have been more than a simple and hence neutral model. Were it to have been the case that what were presented as models were no more than simple models, then it would be possible to argue that they would have embodied and presented, by virtue of that simplicity, an informed neutrality. While it is always possible to respond to this position by arguing that neutrality is never just neutral, that would be to miss the point. Their work eschews the possibility of neutrality, both in itself and in the sense of a neutral representation of that which is in itself not neutral. The impossibility of neutrality within the work of these objects is provided by the presence of repetition or doubling; a provision whose consequence is that the apparent neutrality of the functioning model is itself repositioned by the attempted positing of any founding neutrality being seen to founder. As a direct consequence the actual specificity of the art work's work will have a critical function.[5] Indeed, it will be in terms of the actual emergence of critique — how it is opened up — that it will become possible to identify a specific politics of art practice.

What is important to note here is not the non-reduction itself but the opening that takes place with it, and what is sanctioned by this irreducibility. With that opening it will have been recognised that such a reduction was never in fact possible. This will be the affirmation of the event taking place after the event. Once more the significant related point is that they are not functional objects with further contingent determinations. A different temporal setup is at work, one enjoining a certain necessity. However, if primacy were given to one formulation of irreducibility — the formulation that privileged the 'apart', thereby failing to understand that it was necessarily interrelated to the 'a part' — then there would be a privileging of destruction (and with it, as has already been suggested, the enacting of the metaphysics of destruction). Furthermore, it would mean ignoring the primordiality of relation and that the actual force of the work would have been effaced. Any attempt to present that force will demand that careful attention is given to the relation established by the irreducible. Once again, this is a possibility that is precluded by taking destruction to be an end in itself. Ultimately destruction amounts to no more than the affirmation of negativity and impossibility; in other words the affirmation of the inescapability of the *via negativa*. This is not to argue that in the move away from an aesthetics of metaphysical destruction, the place of negativity and impossibility have been overcome; on the contrary, they will have been maintained. Negativity will have been incorporated as a moment, a flicker within detail, while impossibility enters into a relation by forming part of the apparent paradox of impossible possibility. Here, both as a mode of procedure and as a mode of thinking, it has been replaced by repetition; an-other repetition. Indeed it is a repetition whose presence is necessarily articulated in terms of the logic of the a part/apart. What distinguishes this repetition, and thus what makes it an-other possibility for repetition, is that there is no sequence; therefore what remains is the effective abeyance of both the temporality and ontology of teleology. The presentation and its repetition — perhaps the giving and the giving again — occur at the same time. Part of the inherent complexity of this is that its being effective will only ever be recognised retrospectively. With retrospective temporality not only is there a constitution of the occurrence with the frame set by the event, but there is equally the enforced presence of the temporality of interpretation. Both of these possibilities are the result of an iterative reworking; namely a productive and therefore a workful repetition.

While Langlands & Bell do not allude to repetition as such, they are alert to the potential stemming from that conception of irreducibility in which what is presented will have already been positioned beyond the purview of transgression. Repetition allows another response to the law since it allows for the creation of a space beyond the determinations — both positive and negative — of prediction. As a result, displacing the interplay of transgression and privation will entail that overcoming of the negative which will itself work beyond the counter move of negation.

> Essentially . . . we perceive the work of sculpture which tends to subvert function rather
> than simply reinforcing it. The role of say, a chair, as a familiar, miniature architectural
> space is significant within the framework of what we are trying to achieve.[6]

What must be maintained here is the copresence of the determined and the yet to be determined; their copresence must be taken as forming a constitutive part of the work's work. What should not be overlooked, of course, is that it is the object's material presence that allows it to maintain this anoriginally complex site. Now, even though it is the retention of the chair, table or architectural model as what they are that enables them to work beyond the confines of chair, table and model taken as the simple occurrence, this still leaves open the question of the opening (the opening pertaining here, for example, to what they as artists are, in their own words, 'trying to achieve'). It is not sufficient to argue that the chair, table or model are used as the means by which to take up, or even to pose, the interrelated questions of history, place and architecture. The reason is simply that such an argument, once again, neglects this opening and, in neglecting it, eliminates the place of the work's work. It turns the objects into instruments thereby failing to identify the importance of the founding repetition; a repetition enacted through the logic of the a part/apart. Materiality is essential precisely because it is the matter of the occurrence that provides the possibility of the further enactment. It will be an enactment that will have taken the work further at the same time as the occurrence is enacted. The materiality is worked, and thus reworked, within the movement proper to the temporality of interpretation. (Again it will be within that temporal scheme that the event is released.) Here, therefore, matter bears the repetition. What is retained as open is a space — the 'place' constructed by apart/a part allowing the presentation of the already interrelated presentation of the fields of history and politics. The interrelation is itself complex as it takes place both within the fields themselves as well as with the object's work.

A fundamental part of the interpretive move at work here figures in the distinction — a distinction being maintained in this work's work — between a conception of interpretation that is structured by representation and one in which repetition provides the way; the interpretive way to the work. Representation would turn the works in question into examples or instruments. Utility would be the interpretive drive. Instrumentality and utility, however, have a price. Positioning the objects in the way — allowing them to be positioned by the interpretive dominance of representation — brings about the closure of the work, and with it the constitutive move from occurrence to event becomes possible. This closure should not be understood as an interpretive or semantic claim where the claim's force resided in the closing off of the possibility of further and different interpretations or meanings. It is rather that the closure in question is the effacing or denial of the possibility of the work having its own work; and therefore what is, *au fond*, being denied is the inherent specificity of the ontology of the art object. In sum, in its most straightforward formulation, what is given as a representation works towards the effacing of the very materiality that is the place (thus the site) of the event's work. Representation as the interpretive frame enacts the abnegation of the event. And yet what must be retained is the object's presentation; its occurrence.

## Works

In works such as *Conversation Seat*, *Interlocking Chairs* and *Adjoining Rooms*, the actual possibility of their existence as objects of interpretation — though this is a point also made as part of their interpretation — is constructed by the space opened by the insistent presence of matter. In other words it is only the presence of the table and chair that marks the additional presence. This addition, which is neither an addition nor a supplement, is given within repetition. (The logic of the apart/a part works within the complex of repetition.) The seat and the chairs open the possibility of interpretation at that moment where, despite existing as a chair or a seat, they are never just a chair or simply a seat; a part and apart. The 'neither' here will mean that what plays a determining role in understanding the work of the chair or the seat — the particular chair and seat within the works *Conversation Seat* and *Interlocking Chairs* — is the opening enacted by the apart/a part. The repetition occurs insofar as that which holds this opening — holds it as open — is a seat or a chair. Even though they are given again and anew, the twofold movement occurs at the same time; its retroactive recovery is, as has been indicated, the constitution of the given as an event within the process of interpretation. Once more this is the reason why there are not two occurrences (let alone two events), one preceding the other. It is rather that what occurs — that which is given for interpretation — emerges as already complex. At work here is the interplay of materiality and repetition. This reiterates the point advanced above, namely that the presence of a founding irreducibility indicates that while the irreducible is recovered in an act of interpretation — a recovery which is itself possible because of the temporality of interpretation — irreducibility is not a semantic setup but is ontological in nature.

What is allowed by these chairs, therefore, is an-other site of interpretation. The chairs house within their seats models of architectural sites. What characterises these sites is, in general, that they are places of negotiation and political process. Deployed within these modelled sites will be a seating — the positioning of agents within the site — that creates and structures a specific space. Enacted by these seats, therefore — enacted in the reality of their being seats — is the affirmed recognition of the always already present construction of space. The presentation of space as always having been constructed does not, however, take the form of a didactic, aesthetic exercise. It is rather the fact that because these chairs are part of an installed site, and thus because they are part of that which creates the site, they are therefore already incorporated in space's construction. They attest to the impossibility of the neutrality of space by *already* occupying and constructing a specific space. Here the work of construction holds space as that which is deployed within the abeyance of the inside/outside opposition, the chairs' own work of construction brings to the fore that element of their work which enacts the destruction of an enforcing neutrality. With the chairs and with their positing of the seat of power (a doubled seat that is no longer simply ironic even though a certain irony is retained) the productive copresence of matter and repetition opens up the possibility for a reconsideration of spacing. It may be that with this possibility the possibility for art, within this domain, attains its end. With this end what comes to be sanctioned is not the positing of a gesture within the work that envisages an end — and here end would have to be thought of in terms of a temporality of reconciliation — but in holding to the question as that which is repositioned as an integral part of the work's work, what is then opened up is precisely the possibility of taking up the question without its traditional determinations. With these seats it is the site itself that, in being enacted by the seat, allows for an-other consideration.

The complex generated by the interplay of materiality and repetition figures in a more detailed way in their recent (1990) installation at the Fondation pour l'Architecture in Brussels. This installation included a number of works one of which was *Surrounding Time*.

It goes without saying that part of the difficulty here is that, notwithstanding the explanatory force of a detailed description of this work, it remains the case that part of what has to be developed is a tradition in which the interpretive language (and with it the requisite concepts and categories) proper to installations finds a sustained place. It is because of this need — a need that must always be linked to an understanding of what it is that art can accomplish — that the separation of the occurrence into its constitutive elements is problematic. Problems emerge, for example, in taking an element out of context, or failing to recognise its place within the construction of the internal space, since what such moves overlook is the fact that the relation between the constitutive elements is itself an integral part of the object of interpretation. Space within the relation does not house the component parts. On the contrary it is the interplay of these constructed 'parts' that, in forming the constitutive elements of the installation, construct space. Neither site nor installation are in space. They allow for a spacing that is part of the object's being. Space therefore not only forms an integral part of the installation, it is insistently there as a constitutive and thus constituting part of the installation's own work. The traditional concepts of space, despite their range, nonetheless seem to be inadequate with regard to the complex task that arises from having positioned the occurrence — the installation for example — as an object of interpretation. However, even taking the problems involved into consideration, in order that another move be made it is essential to take a risk. The imposition of this limit not only occasions risk, it is the risk in being taken which signals philosophy's attempt to respond to the contemporary force of the art work.

*Surrounding Time* consists of three framed models. The buildings in question are 'The Glaverbal HQ', 'La Maison de Force' and 'The Colosseum'. And yet there is a fundamental element of the term 'model' that is far from adequate for grasping what is at play here. In a general sense the problem emerges in the move from noun to verb. The models do not model as such. There is no simple outside. It is, rather, that they can be said to display. And yet the problematic element of this setup comes to be compounded for this is not a simple display. What is presented is not, straightforwardly, a series of models. It is rather that, here, models display. What, then, is being displayed? The initial answer is social space. Here it is space within, and as, buildings which have an ineliminable relation to bureaucracy and power. Framing what are initially divisions that construct internal space, the framed presence of these divisions — the surrounded space — open up by displaying within the models the necessary interarticulation of space and power. It is moreover an interarticulation that has its own developments, its own specificity. The specificity in question is the continuity of place (the place of place) within the history of European architecture. Here it is displayed; the conditions of display are, of course, the move from occurrence — the doubling — that is occasioned by the event. The repetition of the model — a move sanctioned by the occurrence, the insistent and hence ineliminable material presence — in resisting the projection of neutrality, works to sunder the possibility of an initial neutrality that would be retained, if all that was taken to be displayed were models.

*Langlands & Bell*, Surrounding Time, *1990, installation view, Saatchi Collection, London, MDF, beech, poplar, wood products, glass, AC lacquer (reproduced courtesy of Glenn Scott Wright, Contemporary Art)*

The move from model to display therefore must be necessarily related to the general displacement of representation; a displacing in which its place is ceded to repetition. With this move it can no longer be maintained that the display represents the model. The model, however, figures within the display as the site of repetition. The move marks the presence of the logic of the apart/a part.[7] In this instance there is, with the emergence of display, a necessary transformation. The corresponding position also needs to be noted, since it is also the case that there can be no initial display for all that could be displayed (assuming that the force of what is involved here occurs in the move from noun to verb) would be a model. The consequence as well as the implicit premise of both these points is the posited centrality of the material; materiality as such. What this means is that it is the materiality of the models that forces an opening in which the matter of the object gives rise to that element of the event which is not purely material, namely the move from model to display. This move is the interplay of the work of materiality and the logic of the a part/apart. Once more the move involves the complex directionality and temporality of interpretation. It would be a mistake to take such a move as providing the totality of the answer to the question: what do the models display? What it does, however, is provide that question with the conditions of possibility for its answer. Yet it remains the case that the general answer to the question of display must necessarily involve the detail — the specificity — of the object in question. The frames contain specific models. Even though they are displayed, the move from model to display opens the space within the frame. The space in question is neither the posited nor the assumed spatiality of the object; it is, rather, that it should be taken as at work in the place where the model is no longer the model of, for example, 'The Colosseum', but where 'The Colosseum' enacts and presents both a determining effect as well as presenting itself as the site of that determination. What will have to be taken up is the nature of this twofold presence. Nonetheless, what it entails here is that with 'The Colosseum' — the model of 'The Colosseum' — there is a complex display. It is the interplay of these determinations which will need to be pursued.

In the first place the display is of 'The Colosseum'; on a straightforward level that is the building which is modelled. In the second place the model forms part of a large set of relations that work to comprise the installation. The internal spacing of the model is already mediated, therefore, by the other and already present spatial relations that it works to sustain and thus of which it (the now plural 'it') already forms a part. In the third place the result, even though it is a result that is simultaneous with the occurrence, is that 'The Colosseum' — both the named work and the building of which this is the ostensible model — displays the place of architecture's necessary incorporation of an always already present determination of function. In other words rather than allowing function to be posited as such, and as though that positing were all that was needed to locate the specificity of the building, the specific function is dramatised in being displayed. This evocation of the necessity of the specific has an automatic and important consequence. Function, rather than being taken as an abstract and to that extent universal term yielding a singular and therefore unequivocal

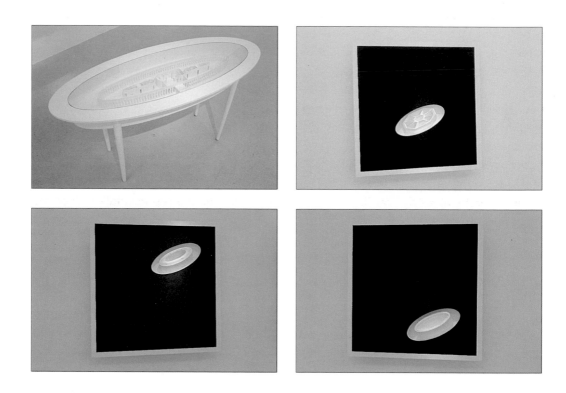

*Langlands & Bell, details of* Surrounding Time, *1990: 'Brussels University' and 'La Maison de Force' (above); 'The Glaverbal HQ' and 'The Colosseum' (below) (reproduced courtesy of Glenn Scott Wright, Contemporary Art)*

evaluation, is allowed that degree of clarity in which what is displayed is the actual function. This allows in the first place the possibility of the retention of functionality but in terms of its being incorporated within another project, while indicating in the second place that the project in question will necessitate an-other and radically different architecture. The interplay of history, space and power that is displayed by 'The Colosseum' works to establish limits. A fundamental part of what is established by these limits concerns both the articulation of critique and the refusal of a programmatic utopian plan. The final, though fundamental, point is that it has all of these determinations occurring and thus finding a place at one and the same time. The time in question will, once more, attest to the presence of anoriginal complexity. The presence — and here it is both an insistent and productive presence — of a founding complexity works to indicate that what is involved is not semantic overdetermination. After all, it is not that the object's mode of being is undecidable; it is, rather, and more importantly, that the object is complex. Semantic undecidability will always be parasitic upon a specific ontological setup. In sum, complexity is not semantic as such, it refers on the contrary to the ontology of the object. Semantic or interpretive undecidability has its own necessary conditions of possibility.

Historical buildings figure in a number of their works. The presentation nearly always involves a plan or model that is itself either integrated into a chair or framed as a model. In both cases the description of integration and framing is inadequate in that it is the position of the architectural presence within an object outside of that presence that mediates the former, thereby allowing it to display. The display is no longer a representation since the placement of the model denies it its capacity to model and therefore of the model to represent, and thus just to be a representation of the actual building. It must not be forgotten, however, that there is also a model of a well known building. The model means that the building is present. The significant point is that in being repeated the model moves from being itself, where its meaning would be defined in terms of what the original building actually meant, to being a display where the attribution of meaning is going to involve the very spatiality that has been created by repetition. It is only if this latter move is seen as in fact taking place, that it becomes possible to argue that what is displayed is the fact of the interarticulation of space and power. Having come this far it is essential to remain with the specificity of work. In this instance, however, that specificity must be another mediation. Here, rather than taking the determinations of function as central, it is the object's own aesthetic quality that must be allowed a determining role; and it is this quality that is opened up by their being art objects. In other words, it is only because the objects are presented within the twofold articulation of the logic of the apart/a part that it becomes possible to question the relationship between their aesthetic quality and their work.

## Aesthetic Objects

What could provisionally be described as the problem of aestheticisation of the art work is to be understood here as involving the nature of the link to beauty, and with that link the necessary presence of the pleasure (or displeasure) provided by the object. While not describing it as a problem as such, Marie-Ange Brayer identifies what to her is a 'paradox' in their work:

> These works hinge on a paradox. They question architecture as an ideology, but are, at the same time, extremely refined formal objects. The eye, which is subjected to the system that governs the plan, is also solicited for its pure aesthetic pleasure.[8]

The implicit suggestion that is contained in this description pertains to the possible loss that may be occasioned by beauty. In what sense, therefore, is the description of the work as paradoxical in any sense accurate? Furthermore what, both generally and specifically, would be the consequence of the possible accuracy of this description? In responding to these questions it will be possible to pursue the limits of their work. Limits, however, should not be understood as the identification of failure occasioned by critique; indeed the actual practice of the work necessarily brings limits with it. Part of the activity of critique is the identification of the work's own activity and thus of the identification of the work's limits. The productive element within critique is that in establishing these limits, the possibility is set up of a further opening and thus of another adventure within the visual arts.

The paradox identified above hinges on the possibility that the attraction of the objects — what has already been described here in terms of an elegant austerity — blunts their critical edge, and therefore at the very extreme would work to undermine the project that comprises the work's work. There are two levels of response to this possibility. The first concerns what could be formulated in terms of the absence of necessity, and the second as the necessity of the provisional. These two levels are, of course, interrelated; moreover their actual formulation works to check whatever force there could have been attributed to paradox. As a beginning, however, the 'paradox' — what is formulated as paradox without there necessarily being an actual paradox as such — needs to be pursued. What is at work within the formulation of paradox is the possibility that the intended power of the work (power here should be understood in terms of the critical possibility already identified as emerging out of the logic of the apart/a part) would come to be either denied or effaced because of the presence of paradox. What endures as the implicit premise that structures this possibility is an either/or in which either their work will have this critical dimension in all its exactitude and consequence, or such a dimension will be completely absent. In other words, that it is either necessarily present or necessarily absent. It would seem, however, that it is precisely this possibility — the absolutising effect of an all-encompassing either/or — that needs to be questioned. In questioning it what should nonetheless neither be denied nor allowed to be too distant a possibility is that, even if the language of the either/or ceases to be appropriate, it still could have been the case that there was a diminution of the work's effect brought about through the activity of aetheticising. There will always be the real possibility that the aestheticising effect may come to play a significant role in the evaluation not just of their work but, more importantly, of the work's work. What remains as the task in addition to clarifying the presence of aestheticising is thinking of its possible intrusion independently of the possibilities set up by the either/or.

The response to what was identified as a 'paradox' is to be found in its formulation. Part of the threat that is brought about by the object taking on the task of giving pleasure is that it will be identified with that which gives pleasure. The eye will be 'solicited' for that alone. Once more it is the absolute nature of this possibility that determines the extent of the threat. However, in the case of Langlands & Bell it could be argued that it is the very possibility of aesthetic pleasure — the solicitation of the eye — that enables, in part, their work to have the critical success that it does. In other words it is the possibility of aestheticising that while attracting the eye — attracting by offering a certain neutrality and thus formality — allows that attraction to present a work that once the eye is held the work is such that the object's formality checks the possibility of any neutrality. Aestheticising becomes part of the work's work. It should be added, of course, that the move from formality to the checking of neutrality is made within the activity of interpretation. Universalising the claim by arguing for its essential necessity therefore will itself be checked both by the nature of the object in question and by the necessity of the provisional and the pragmatic within the activity of interpretation.

Limits are therefore set by allowing the works to work. The interplay between formality and beauty — when understood as the possibility opened up by that construal of modernism that begins with Kant — would only be allowed to dominate if the complexity engendered and sustained by the apart/a part were either precluded or overlooked.[9] The fact that both are possible and that the work's work could always be forgotten is not the basis of an argument against the works as such. These possibilities should be linked to the impossibility that a work's force could be completely unidirectional and therefore the 'same' for all (in sum the necessary impossibility of necessity). Once the work is allowed its inherent complexity, and furthermore once the 'all' is allowed, the absolute within art gives way to its other possibility. Here, otherness is connected to the strategic. For any strategy, all that can be universalised is its inherently pragmatic nature. Here, with the work of Langlands & Bell, the *pragma* takes on a necessarily political dimension.

*Christian Boltanski,* Leçons des Ténèbres, *1987 (above), black and white photographs, metal lamps, installation view, Kunsthalle, Bern;* Ombres, *1984 (below), wood, cardboard, tin, cork, wire, projector, fans, dimensions variable, installation view (reproduced courtesy of Lisson Gallery, London)*

# Installed Memory: Christian Boltanski

Writing on Boltanski will necessitate detours; undertaken here, in part, by working through figures. It is as though the presentation of the work needs to be staged. And yet this description is not in itself completely accurate since what must, in the end, be provided is what the work itself stages; a staging in relation to figures. There is an attendant difficulty. What is staged by the work and thus what it sets up, turns around a series of concerns that are sufficiently close that they may remain unnoticed. The presentation of a number of possible detours, in working through them, will occasion an essential distancing to take place. Work will yield the works in question. It will be in allowing what is distanced to emerge such that the closeness of the distanced, at times its actual intimacy, will be shown, and thus will be able to figure. The interplay of nearness and distance — a play that will have already been reworked by the complex temporality of interpretation — will figure within the multiple determinations of memory. What will have to be shown, having made these detours, is that the place of Boltanski's work — the internality and the specificity of the work itself — is given by what has already been identified as the object-in-question. It is the object thus conceived that sets and determines the possible forms of the question of memory. (Here it will be a question mediated by a recasting of the structure and expectations of knowledge.) As a beginning, however, it is memory, its being as a question, that comprises the work's work. Memory, while central to this undertaking, will emerge as a site of intensity given by the difficulty of the relationship between experience and historical time. While there are other sites in which this relation plays a significant role, memory brings with it the interplay of actual experience, what amounts to the reality of remembering, as well as the complex determinations provided by the subject matter of memory, namely that which is given to be remembered, and finally the conditions that work to construct memory. Memory already figures. It is already taking place.

**Memory, Tragedy**

Here it cannot be just memory since its ineluctable quality can be too readily admitted. It is rather that with these works there is the work of memory; the specific modality of its being present. While it is almost impossible to avoid using the singular and of having to take up 'memory' as though it were a single activity with carefully defined determinations, it should be recognised that memory involves a plurality. Indeed it is possible to go further since the plurality at work within it rehearses the varying determinations given by the interplay of experience and historical time. In accepting the need to start with the singular — with the work of memory — the question that immediately arises will concern how that work is to be understood. Memory will need its place, not just its place in history but within the history that memory brings with it; a history that incorporates what it is that is given to be remembered. It will be with what is given that memory will be linked to the effective presence of experience.

As a procedural move it is possible to start with a question: why, today, should there be a concern with memory? The immediate answer would seem to be that memory is, to an extent, already catered for; from the monument that commemorates the dead, allowing them to be remembered, to the passing on of familial stories of the activities of relatives now gone, the latter mediated by the photographic album that now plays such a vital part in family life, memory and the work of memory seem to endure. Moreover, even with non-family based groupings, memory works to provide and to sustain that group's history and to that extent, therefore, its identity. Memory, or rather the work of memory — be it linked to an actual task or an envisaged one — seems to play a pervasive and binding role. Even though remembrance within these formulations lacks specificity it is still possible to ask why memory would be a question? What makes the question seem to insist is linked to its being posed today; in other words its demand as a question pivots around the force of 'today'.[1] This day — 'today' — is not the day whose presence is marked by a date and yet of course it is a day that will always be able to be dated. Memory and its presence 'today' demand that the day be taken up; the day can no longer be accepted either in its own terms or as simply given. The force of 'today' cannot be escaped. What occurs 'today'? Asking this questions brings two further considerations into play. The first is the necessity to give a philosophical description of 'today'. The second is to recognise that part of that description will provide an essential element of the construction of modernity; the latter, once infused with the former, needs to be understood as the contemporary place of writing.

What will, however, check the traditionally modernist aspirations of this construction is the further recognition that philosophy has no outside place from which to operate or describe. What must always be remembered, therefore, is the necessity for philosophy to work with, and within, its own recognition of the fact that it is already part of the activity that it seeks to describe. (This is philosophical realism.) The already implicated place of philosophy not only signals the impossibility of a metaphysics of destruction, but it is also another formulation of the ineliminable and thus primordial presence of relation. The All — the figure of totality — cannot be constructed, and yet working with this recognition need not give rise to either the pathos of the aporetic — a pathos made even more emphatic by its having been naturalised — or the projected inescapability of the *via negativa*. There will need to be a different understanding of this impossibility. The impossible All will need another setting. In other words there will need to be a way of escaping the nihilism that arises once the only response to this projected impossibility is the inevitability of working with, and within, pathos, aporia and negation. As was suggested, part of what gives this nihilism its force is that, with such a response, the All is naturalised such that the response has to be inevitable.

If totality is that which includes all that is given such that all of its elements are taken as already part of the All, then amongst other possibilities the All becomes a figure of God. Regardless of the detail that is given to the varying formulations of the present, it is, in general, marked by the death of this God; in sum the impossibility as well as the implausibility of the All. Moreover, once it is possible to argue for the death of God, then this will not be an argument about belief — a claim that would fall within the province of theology rather than philosophy — but would rather amount to an argument about the death of philosophy's God of totality and absorption. Consequently, prior to returning to 'today' — to memory occurring and constituting the place of 'today' — it is the death of this philosophical God that must be of concern. The concern here is not a minor one since the consequence of accepting the argument for this God's death redefines the present in different terms. One of the ways in which it comes to be defined is, as has been suggested, in terms that are both aporetic and negative; within this definition aporia and negation are both privileged and naturalised. Indeed what will be seen is that, to the extent that the present is viewed in these terms, then such a view is itself only possible because it is taken as the only response to God's death. With naturalisation, commitment to one state of affairs will entail commitment — now negated — to the other. This death, which is itself one way of understanding the announced impossibility of totality and the absorbing All, can be construed as entailing that 'today' lacks the possibility of unity and synthesis — remembering that the lack and the disunity will be given by the founding possibility of the All — such that it has become the place of tragedy. As a consequence what would play a determining and defining role within the contemporary would be the inescapable presence of tragedy. What would therefore endure at the present — as the present — is what could be described as the figure of tragedy; the haunting and immovable presence of the lack of reconciliation.[2]

In pursuing this argument, the figure of tragedy that determines the contemporary would be the necessary presence of irreconcilability. Once again it is not irreconcilability as such; to think that it were would in this instance misunderstand the process and the force of naturalisation. Here irreconcilability is given by the All — the All that was actually or potentially there — having been sundered. The reason for the impossibility of reconciliation — an impossibility occurring in and thus determining the present — would be the absence of that in which (or in whom) differences were both identified and overcome. If God is the one in whom in all differences and conflicts are finally resolved, then God's death may turn the present into the site in which the figure of tragedy plays an inevitable role. However as God here is neither the God of theology nor of prayer, the question of the present — 'today' — has to be thought beyond the opposition between atheism and theism. It is rather that God will name the possibility of any final reconciliation. Moreover, once the reciprocity in this formulation is recognised, then it will be that the actual (or futural) possibility of this God is what allows for the continual and therefore conflictual lack of reconciliation. In other words the figure of tragedy and the

God of ultimate reconciliation are necessarily interrelated. One cannot exist without the other; one is quite literally unthinkable without the other. As such God becomes a name for a final reconciliation or absorption. God is both finality and totality. As such God is either an enduring absence or a futural possibility. God's death ends the possibility of peace by stripping the present of any hope by locating hope in the future. Hope, therefore, within this setup, could not be a condition of the present.

And yet, even in pursuing the structure of this argument, there is no need to stay with the language of God and the death of God. (Indeed, ultimately the argument is about time — the philosophy of historical time — and this accounts for why here there is the work of figures.) Once God is understood no longer as the divine but as a name or figure for the final unifying force in which conflict is ultimately resolved and reconciliation reached, then it is possible to replace the figure of God with other names/figures all of which would bring the same intention with them. It would be thus that the nation, perhaps even the state, could stand for this God by providing the unifying and synthesising All. In each instance what such a replacement would suggest is that it is the construal of nation or state as providing a synthesising totality that will obviate the threat of a perpetual lack of reconciliation. Here, there would be the direct political programme inaugurated by the unifying God and thus potentially sundered by God's death. Again, still working within the frame of this argument, to announce the impossibility of such a conception of nation or state is to announce the enduring presence of a conflictual irreconcilability and thus to announce, *de facto,* the perpetual presence of the figure of tragedy. As has already been suggested the important point here however is neither God's death nor the figure of tragedy taken as ends in themselves but their necessary symbiosis. As such the concern with irreconcilability and the threat of the figure of tragedy are themselves only possible because of this God's death; neither tragedy nor pathos nor the aporetic exist in and of themselves. Accepting such a setup turns the present — 'today' — into a site marked, determined and structured by mourning, by loss. It is because of the interdependence between irreconcilability and totality that it will be possible to provide a site for aspects of Boltanski's work.

The importance of establishing the relationship of dependence between, on the hand the All — the figure of God — and pathos and the aporetic on the other, is that not only does it allow for a particular formulation of the present, it also implicates these two possibilities as given with that formulation. The entire setup amounts to a complex either/ or. The importance of Boltanski's work is that while it is located within the recognition of the impossibility of the All, that recognition is not articulated within the terms set by this either/or. What is involved here, therefore, is another understanding of 'today' and thus a different conception of the present, and with it another take on the work of memory. Indeed it will become possible to locate Boltanski's work at this precise point. It will be a point, moreover, that will involve affirmation and differentiation rather than negation and impossibility.

## Tragedy, Memory

Here it will be essential to take up another detour. In the first instance it was the turn within the present from memory to tragedy; a turn within a particular argument in which the present became a site marked by a necessary irreconcilability in which God's death — remembering the detailed specificity of this God — left the future as an empty space traversed by an insistent loss occasioning mourning and whose overcoming lay in the possibility of utopian projections. This will be, as has been indicated though is yet to be shown, a position countered by the work of specific works. The next detour will link the question of memory not to tragedy but to a specific project of annihilation and thus to the tragedy of its occurrence. It is a project that can be taken as having a determining effect 'today'. In turning in this way, the necessity of the day is still maintained and held in its becoming more than the given day. The difference however will be given by the quality attributed to the present. Part of that quality will be the temporality that it presupposes.

There cannot be a simple move. Nor can there be an emphatic jump from the project of annihilation to memory. There must be a turning. In the turn the specificity of that project comes to be stated. No longer a figure that haunts as an abstraction; here the annihilation is real. It has dates. And yet it is far more than occurrences bearing dates, thus far more real than any dated reality. The annihilation — and it must be continually wondered which word of this order is the most appropriate — is there for thinking, there for history and therefore has to be there within the deployment of what the dominant project of European philosophy has always deployed in its formulations and understanding of both history and thinking. What must be allowed to bear on this undertaking, even if only present as a need as that which needs to be considered — are two interrelated questions. What will need to be asked in the first place is: to what the extent is this already determined thinking implicated in the Shoah? And in the second place: are the resources and modes of presentation that the already determined brings with it able, in their own terms, to think the Shoah? What needs to be understood is that there is no straightforward answer to these questions. They need to be investigated, taken up and thus worked through as questions. An immediate response would be im-mediate and thus lacking the inescapable mediation of questioning.

Any future philosophical thinking, and with it any art practice that brings with it the problematic stakes of memory — understood as memorialisation of/for the dead — is constrained by this 'massacre'.[3] In a passionate yet scrupulously argued work Emil Fackenheim has argued that with the Shoah the continuity of tradition is broken. As a 'novum in world history' what is demanded is the recognition that what occurred cannot be assimilated to any existing calendar. It must find a place but always in being more. The radical force of this is that it must, in part, remain unredeemed. As Fackenheim has argued, 'the unredeemed anguish of Auschwitz must be ever-present with us, even as it is past for us'.[4] It is the twofold of being *ever present* and *ever past*, where both occur at the same time that turns this time — the present, 'today' — into a complex and works to indicate why the Shoah must have the status of that which, while having its own particularity — to use Fackenheim's terms 'a novum' — is also, at the same time, not isolated. (Indeed, its very lack of isolation is indicated by the way in which the Shoah plays a determining role at the present.) To the extent that this description is accepted then the conventions of memory are challenged by the necessity of a remembering that resists absorption and assimilation (what Fackenheim means by 'unredeemed'), while at the same time allowing the work of memory to take place. This does not mean, however, that henceforth the scene is set for another remembering as though the form and practice of that remembering is already at hand. The alterity in question is more insistent as well as being more elusive. What is set is the question of what henceforth will it mean to remember? How 'today' are the dead to be commemorated? Significant elements of Boltanski's work figure in that they can be understood as the continual take-up of these questions. In having this as their project what is given in addition is a site of evaluation and judgement. Evaluation, however, will always need to be linked to the particularity of the project.

It will be the enjoined necessity and therefore the real possibility of this other remembering — present here as questions — that will work to check the aporia of irreconcilability and thus the present in which it is situated and to which it gives rise. By real possibility what is intended is a description of a state of affairs that is neither speculative nor the subject of choice. The reality is an insistent presence figuring within the contemporary and to that extent it can be taken — perhaps in the place of tragedy — as the figure of modernity. The Shoah therefore repositions the art of memory away from the possibility of redeeming what took place. The absence of redemption here is the absence of that position that would attempt to include — perhaps reinclude — what took place within a final and all-inclusive conception of historical time. There is a necessity, and it will be a necessity for memory that, in the first place, the Shoah should remain unredeemed — by what right or in whose name would (or could) such a redemptive occurrence be enacted? Who would forgive? For whom would there be grace? In the second place that memory would become linked to specific practices. The practices in question would be oriented around a vigilance which in being maintained, at the present, can be understood as the activity of present remembrance. This form of remembrance brings another determination of time into play. With these actions another present comes to be formulated.

In general the monument recalls the past; it may even stand for it. It is the marker in the present of that which has occurred. It recalls. However such a clearly differentiated division and inclusion is located within a temporal sequence that is at most only mildly disturbed by what has passed into the present. Indeed, the continuity of tradition demands that the process of incorporation involves a relatively unproblematic subsumption. While most acts play a determining role in what occurs in their wake, here the determination affects how the sequence is itself to be understood. Two consequences arise here. They are the results not just of the problem of the monument but of the situation of that problematic site in a setup that is itself determined by the impossibility of redemption; more emphatically perhaps by the necessity not to redeem. With this necessity there is the enjoined need to think beyond the continuity of tradition. The first consequence is that the nature of the determination itself resists any automatic reincorporation back into the tradition of the monument, while the second is that what is to be remembered must — leaving to one side the horror of detail — be left open. It is possible to suggest, following the work of Lacoue-Labarthe and Fackenheim, that what was lost included a particular modality of thinking. With the loss neither mourning nor melancholia become options; rather, what arises is another fundamentally different call upon thinking.

## Memory's Practice

Having made these detours and accepting their hesitancy there are nonetheless two types of work that they serve to situate. The first are the works involving shadows, for example *Ombres* and *Les Bougies*, and the second is comprised of the monumental work beginning with various works in 1985 and continuing up to and after the more recent *Les Suisses morts*. These two domains of artistic activity are obviously interrelated. And as the same works — the same installed sites recognised as the same by retaining the identical name — may have had different settings, the nature of the setting must also be allowed to play a role in the constitution of the site (sites understood as already included with the locus of interpretation). The complexity of the work and the way in which the problem of memory figures has always engaged an important critical response. Here the significance of that response will lie, in the instance to be considered, in its failure to grasp the way in which aspects of Boltanski's work attest to the presence of an actual problem with memory and thus with the practice of commemoration. Actuality is central. What is near must, though always with an inevitable distancing, emerge as playing a constructive role at the present.

In writing of Boltanski's work Michael Newman locates it within the possibility for memory that has been opened by the Shoah.[5] There is nonetheless a difficulty with his approach. It is a difficulty that, as will be argued, does not hinge on the structure of argument, but rather on the conception of the present at work within it. His detailed interpretation of Boltanski attempts to plot the limit of that work. Part of this interpretive engagement involves a critique of the use of lights and lamps in those works by Boltanski that can be grouped under the heading 'Monuments'. The lamps for Newman refer to a religious context. While this opens up a number of possibilities the nature of such references is interpreted by Newman not as the 'affirmation of art as a post-Enlightenment replacement for religion'; it is rather that they

> . . . mark, on the one hand, the absence of the religious community as a community of mourning, of co-memoration, and on the other, the trace of an event beyond or resistant to recall.[6]

*Christian Boltanski*, L'Ange d'alliance, *1986, installation view, Musée de l'Archéologie Méditerranéenne, Centre de la Vieille Charité, Marseille, copper, feathers, projector, metal base, dimensions variable (reproduced courtesy of Lisson Gallery, London)*

The 'Monuments' are located in other words within the absence of community and the presence of an absolute loss. By taking up some of Boltanski's comments about his work of this period Newman interprets this loss as referring more or less exclusively to Boltanski's own childhood and thus by extension to a personal loss of childhood. He goes on to argue that these works which consist of illuminated photographs of faces that have been applied to metal surfaces, such that the faces are in consequence partly blurred and in which the eyes seem to have lost the capacity to hold the viewer's gaze, cannot, by virtue of the particularity of their physical presence, commemorate. For Newman it is precisely the way in which the 'Monuments' are present that disqualifies them from being acts of commemoration. Newman argues that the tenuous nature of the light provided by the lamps means that were the lamps, as he suggests,

> to be extinguished, the work with its memorial images would disappear into total darkness. In the absence of commemoration, the dead are nothing and death, oblivion.[7]

While it is true to argue that the lamps could always go out and thus there is an ever present practical problem, the real critical thrust of Newman's argument lies in the way in which he understands commemoration. Commemoration within his text is presented in a general way such that it refers both to the present — there is an already identified conception of the present within it — and also as setting the conditions of possibility for any commemorative act. The definition given in the argument's presentation indicates why 'Monuments' cannot commemorate; they will be constrained to betray commemoration's actual possibility.

For Newman commemoration is linked to narrative — it is only possible therefore in terms of a narrative that would include and complete. It is for this reason that commemoration is presented as

> the acknowledgement through ritual of an irreducible humanity and the retelling of a story of a life.[8]

Boltanski's monuments, he argues, not only turn the sites of potential memory and commemoration into fetishes but are marked by a fundamental absence. With Boltanski's works — with these 'Monuments' — what are 'missing are the narratives that would accompany the images'. What is intriguing here is that these criticisms would only work if the potential for providing such a narrative were real and that the possibility of 'retelling a life' were an untroubled possibility 'today', at the present and as that which determined the present's own concerns. It is the critique's basis — in other words the specific formulation of the present — that serves to establish its limit.

Since what arises here is the present and thus the work of memory at the present, what is at stake are the actual conditions of memory and thus of commemoration. One of the most daunting problems that occurs because of the Shoah concerns remembering and with it mourning. This problem can take many forms. Specifically, it is at work within contemporary Judaism compounding the divisions between orthodox and liberal Jewry.[9]

More generally it intrudes into the practice of commemoration itself for the straightforward reason that death in the context of the Shoah was oblivion. In many cases generations were murdered such that links are broken and no direct family member may have been left to mourn. With death on this scale who remembers? What do they remember? Whom do they remember? The questions rapidly accumulate forging an insistent necessity — as questions — that determine the contours of the present. Not only do these questions work within the context of the Shoah and its direct aftermath, they also inform the more general problem of memory and commemoration. The reason for this being the case in the aftermath of the Shoah is modernity — here the contemporary site of remembrance. Newman's formulation of the present differs markedly. Consequently, rather than taking these works as signalling the effective presence of what Newman has described as 'the absence of the conditions for co-memoration', they must bring with them another possibility. The possibility is clear. What these works attest to is the problem of commemoration at the present. Rather than being marked out by an absence, the ineliminable fact is that 'today' commemoration will preclude the interplay of complacency and pathos by having to work with — thus also through — the recognition that commemoration 'today' is traversed by a doubt that had not hitherto existed. 'Today' commemoration and remembrance will involve different activities and therefore other forms of work. Each undertaking will be conditioned by the present. It is this recognition that must be pursued through different areas of Boltanski's work; areas yielding other possibilities. The works enact this recognition; they enact it by acting it out as their work. Furthermore, it also works to plot the work's own limits, establishing thereby a different and this time a more regional ground of judgement. In taking up aspects of Boltanski's work, therefore, one of the essential elements will be the attempt to trace both the grounds for as well as the presentation of these other possibilities. Part of this undertaking will involve moving from the restaging of light and truth towards an affirmation of commemoration's presence as an insistent demand occasioning the response of vigilance and the vigilance of response (memory's actative construal). While these aspects can be separated here they will combine to form a complex in which the tradition of knowing and remembering comes to be repositioned. It will be clear, in addition, that this repositioning can bring its own difficulties and problems with it.

One of the most important elements in all of the works to be taken up is their setting. Not only is the setting a type of context, what must not be neglected is the fact that the setting works, as has already been argued, to form an integral part of the work's work. While this point has a necessary generality, here it opens up different works. In a way it may be that the works could be grouped in terms of where they were placed rather than in terms of their specific form. An example would be works placed in a theological context as opposed to works placed in an apparently 'neutral' exhibition space. Perhaps one of the most important settings was the location of *Leçons des Ténèbres* and *Les Anges* in the Chapelle de la Salpetrière in Paris, 1986. While works that form part of *Leçons des*

*Ténèbres* have been located in secular as well as theological or religious sites, the settings bring with them a related though nonetheless different staging of the relationship between light and truth. In both instances the work upstages what had been demanded by the theological as well as the secular setting of that relationship. It would not be an exaggeration to argue that within a structure that demands both light and revelation the centrality attributed to shadows has an immediately disruptive quality. It is this quality that is also present in the more apparently secular setting in which the central role given to the shadow recalls the Platonic cave but with a repositioned priority.[10] Rather than the shadows being the site of deception, it would now be as though the shadows are the site of an illumination given by subjugated light.

What are shadows? What do shadows mean? Shadows, as with a darkness that instructs, resist any automatic assimilation into the language of traditional epistemology. While the site of resistance is clear and its disruptive dimension self-evident, questions still insist. It can still be asked what is it that emerges from the clarity? What is it that is evident? The intriguing aspect of these questions is that they already refer to the process being questioned. In other words these questions are already implicated in what they seek to question. Rather than the traditional critique of epistemology that moves inexorably towards a relativity that is simply epistemology's other possibility, here knowledge and the process of knowing find another setting. What is staged is different. Part of the activity that involves candles or, in the case of *Ombres*, actual lights consists of taking up the nature of the display. The walls on which the reflections are positioned come to form an integral part of the object. The shadows which are cast on the walls are part of the object's presence and yet their presence is, as has already been noted, tenuous and traversed by both an inescapable uncertainty and doubt. Moreover the shadows move. They flicker and dance as that which casts them moves in the wind or in a passing breeze or, more straightfor-wardly, with the passage of time. As with any casting of shadows there is a transformation. What is staged on the wall is not the object before the light source. Light works not only to present but to transform in the process of presenting. The question that arises concerns the status of the original and thus whether or not the transformation is a transformation, and therefore a deceptive presentation of an original which already had a singular and already determined quality. Accepting this question would mean having to accept the possibility that there was both a temporal as well as an evaluative priority in these works. Once the wall, the site of the projection — the surface as stage or place of enactment — is included as part of the object, then what emerges is that the nature of the relationship between light, cast object and shadow takes on a different quality. It is as though these works function as precursors to the 'Monuments' and the other works addressing memory. They provide the frame in which they are to be approached.

The tenuous nature of the shadow — and tenuous needs to be understood as alluding both to the ephemeral quality of the shadow, its immaterial materiality, and its complete dependence on a maintained source of light — opens a series of possibilities. And yet while shadows depend upon light, the work of shadows demands the obscuring of light. Here the obscure does not obscure, nor the darkness hide. Shadows have become the moments and movements of revelation. These are shadow works. What is staged therefore, what is held by the walls on which the immaterial presence of shadows takes on a passing yet real and material presence is another form of presence. It is a different presentation. Part of understanding what defines these presentations will involve the recognition of the part played by time. Even though an important aspect of the time of shadows is linked to the uncertainty generated by the source of light having become precarious, there is a further temporal dimension that must be noted. In this instance it is the time that works within the immaterial materiality; a time that will have become the time of fragility.

The shadows incorporate the wall — the place on which the shadows are cast — as part of the work's work. In addition the wall is, by virtue of its presence, present as a screen or stage; a site of enactment. It bears the shadows which, in being cast, allow for the wall's presence. The presence of the wall as both screen and wall incorporates the site into and as part of the work. What has been created is an entire setting in which the universal and transcendental interplay of truth and representation are distanced by a staging of the illuminating and instructive power of shadows. It is in this precise sense that site attains its specificity. Putting out the lights, be this by a switch that ends the flow of electricity or by extinguishing the candle's flame, need not be interpreted simply in terms of loss and impossibility — an impossibility leading to the aporetic and in that way to the inescapability of the *via negativa* — but as attesting to an inescapable fragility. It is a fragility that is given by the present and by the recognition of the specific impossibility of the All. The time of fragility is the instantiation of a present in which what endures — maintaining the present — is a questioning. However, questioning demands that engagement be maintained and thus action sustained. Fragility mingles with passion as forming the present; this present, 'today'.

Within the context opened by the distancing of the claims of traditional illumination interarticulated with a repositioning of the place of presentation and thus of commemoration, it becomes possible to take up the use of photographs in the 'Monuments' series amongst others. In writing of Boltanski's earlier and gesturally autobiographical work, Lynn Gumpert notes that Boltanski

> created deliberately false reconstructions of both his past and present in the
> attempt to reveal collective memories and mores.[11]

What is not repeated in the 'Monuments' works is the interplay of the true and the false. Indeed it is possible, as has been suggested, to interpret the work with shadows as having repositioned claims about knowledge and that which provides the source of illumination. And yet what Gumpert correctly identifies in his earlier works is a recognition — within and as part of the work — that the possibility of memory and thus of commemoration is no longer given. (What is given even if it is not recognised as such, is that which positions the present as the site where memory and commemoration need to be sustained as questions.) The presence of an ineliminable difficulty will mean that part of the investigation of the possibility of memory and commemoration will itself form part of the process of commemoration.

The faces of the children in *Le Lycée Chases* have a ghostly presence. While the works consist of photographs and thus initially bring with them the supposed reality of photography, they are treated and illuminated such that they almost appear as the living dead. It is not the work of irony that allows them to appear as they are. Jewish children whose annihilation was more or less probable are the dead who live on (the photographs date from 1931). The manner of their death and the move from the particularity of the face, a particularity that becomes all the more intense once the face is attributed a name and thus a personal history, to the reality of mass death in which all vestiges of the particular body vanished, will mean that the nature of that survival is itself uncertain.[12] (Here differing forms of singularity are at work.) The possibility of identifying with a face — of seeing oneself in another — is precluded by the ways in which these faces are presented. There is a division that precludes a complete identification. The works work to exclude the possibility of a complete identification and yet the photographs work to maintain — at the same time and as part of their work — the possibility of a type of identification and a form of connection. They are human faces.[13] And yet within this work their now anonymous presence, while carrying that anonymity, does not vanish into it. The works work against disappearance and therefore against the presentation of dead space. They are not, in other words, completely anonymous. The ways in which the faces are presented could be interpreted as the deferral of full presence, and yet such an interpretation would amount to no more than the other possibility of a complete presentation. Here the work of the photograph neither presents nor does not present, neither holds the actual presentation up nor gives it *in toto*. What will need to be found is another formulation, one working the abeyance of the negative. This possibility lies in what has already emerged in terms of the relationship to the face. It is this point that will have to be pursued.

A start can be made with anonymity; with the unknown face. The face that can be recognised as a face — another face — gives rise to a possible identification. And yet such an identification cannot be thought of as involving a straightforward identity. Two faces are not identical. The level of identification must occur with what the face presents. There is a projected and perhaps hoped for simultaneity in which the presence of an encountered sameness neither results in nor demands identity. In the encounter the face encountered must look back, the face must hold the viewer's eye. In being held — with the eyes holding each other — there is the possibility of identification. With that other face, therefore also in the other face, there resides an identification that may allow, if not sanction, a certain sameness. As has already been indicated the photograph of a face invites this form of identification. Here the invitation while offered is also withdrawn. It is the presence of the two occurring at the same time that accounts here for the work's work.

As faces they sanction identification. They form part and thus are a part of a projected sameness. As that project begins to take place, in allowing for the possible nearness that would result from identification the faces begin to distance themselves. They begin to hold themselves apart from the project and thus projection of identification. Time here is essential since what occurs takes place at the same time; once more what is at work is that specific interplay of ontology and time that signals the presence of anoriginal complexity. What the logic of the apart/a part allows for is a commemoration that recognises the difficulty of memory at the present. What these 'Monuments' present is the enacted presence of this recognition. It is not the only form in which such an enactment can take place; nonetheless, in allowing the question of memory to endure, what is confronted with these works is the insistent work of a questioning that arises from the present and thus from allowing 'today' to bear upon the nature of work. It is clear that what is sustained by this questioning — by the centrality of an ineliminable questioning that becomes the object's work — is what has already been identified as the object-in-question. The extent to which it is possible to link work to questioning is the extent to which the maintenance of the work and its being as an object are present as the continuity of the becoming-object. In other words the continuity of work — the work of an enduring and insistent questioning — in demanding not just an ontological description but being itself already descriptive of a particular ontological (and temporal) setup is, once again, explicable in terms of the becoming-object.

It is possible to extend this analysis by taking up a work of the same period, *Les Suisses morts*. The importance of this work is that while not concerning itself directly with the aftermath of the Shoah — its content is not the Jewish dead — its work involves the recognition that the present is determined by the Shoah, therefore work is situated within the Shoah's aftermath because of that determining presence. This work which consists of the reproduction of the photographs accompanying death notices in Swiss newspapers, raises the problem on the one hand of a potential banalisation of death while one the other there is the threat that the redeployment of a personal notice may have the consequence of rendering death kitsch. Death may have been made banal by the actual personal death having been depersonalised; and, although this depersonalisation brings an obvious personal dimension with it, in the reproduction of the heads out of context and as depersonalised art forms, it may in the process have become kitsch.

One possible response to the threat of banality and the kitsch would be to opt for a form of authenticity and thus for the advocation of an authentic form of remembrance linked to the authentic death. The possibility of such a response obviously hinges on the possibility of authenticity. With the Shoah, in its aftermath, any death in the impossibility of maintaining its privacy — an impossibility which is already there in the necessity, be it cultural or legal, to acknowledge death publicly — enters a realm in which the structural and institutional forms of the interplay of death and remembrance are already determined by that actualisation of mass death. *Les Suisses morts* therefore becomes a reflection on the possibility of commemoration in the age of mass death. Rather than refusing the present or turning the present into a site that can only generate the impossible, there is an attempt here to work through the present. This work, as with other important aspects of Boltanski's undertakings, turns around the recognition of a present marked by a necessary fragility. The recognition, however, rather than occasioning the lament of the aporetic — the putatively inescapable *via negativa* — generates a specific present that becomes the site of work. Boltanski's work brings with it, therefore, an almost affirmative realism; a reality given by holding to the abeyance of redemption.

*Christian Boltanski,* Le Lycée Chases, *1987, detail, black and white photographs, tin frame, tin biscuit boxes, photomechanical prints, metal lamps, installation approximately 120x120x23cm (reproduced courtesy of Lisson Gallery, London)*

*Robert Ryman,* Untitled, *1965, oil on linen, 26x26cm (reproduced courtesy of Pace Wildenstein, New York)*

# Painting as Object: Robert Ryman

There is a tradition in which beauty and simplicity seem to be combined.[1] Within this tradition, the beautiful seems to be present; present and presented with a particular object. Here, as a beginning, with this work it is the white canvas — perhaps the white object — that holds. In being held a supposition comes into play. With its simplicity, that which is present as simple form may be beauty; it may therefore sustain the presence and thus the present harmony that will have already been identified as the beautiful. Within this realm of possibilities — the possibility of the beautiful — questions arise. What is this semblance? What is it that seems? Is there an actual combination of form, beauty and simplicity that holds? How do these paintings work? And yet, of course, to write of 'paintings' may be already to concede that which is from the start problematic, namely the possibility of a universality of strategy that is able to be grouped under and thus gathered up by the proper name Ryman; gathered up and held in other words, by no more than the name. Rather than concentrating on the name, in this instance in the place of its centrality, there will be work. Work will always stand in another position, not in contradistinction to the name but with its distanced retention (a twofold that is itself the mark of a specific abeyance). Work, here within an abstract art form, a form that is already connected to the project of minimalism, is ineliminably linked to the question of the art object by the intensity of the painting's own relation to the project — and thus to the projection — of the pure object.

Art has never been nor has it just become completely self-reflective, if reflexivity is taken as a simple generality. It is rather that art's presence in terms of specific art forms and their link to the question of the object's own being is, in this instance, that which can be taken as structuring this particular undertaking. Even then it will not be art as such but, more specifically, the relation between painting and sculpture that will emerge as central. It will be in terms of this relation that the object-in-question can be identified. In this regard even Ryman's own claims about the reality of his work will need to be reinterpreted. Indeed, the failure of his having attempted to determine in advance how the work is to be addressed, in particular his argument for the centrality of realism in the place of abstraction, needs to be interpreted as further testament to the way the work itself takes the question of its being — the question of its being art — as an integral part of its work.

Here, with the opening up of this authorial limit, there is the necessity to take such a description a step further. With Ryman it is possible to suggest that an essential part of the work's concern — the concern that delimits the specific activity of the work in question — is the question of the object. And yet such a claim looks like a simple tautology — the work is the work that it is. However it will be argued here — an argument rehearsing moves already made — that once that particular claim is stripped of its simply tautological nature, what will emerge is an-other opening, and therefore a different engagement with the question of the object. (Indeed, the tautological can be reformulated as the work is the work that it *does.*) What will be argued however is that the frame, the conjectured site of painting's activity, once taken as involving the necessary incorporation of time, holds the question (a temporalised question intrinsic to the work's work) open as a site of activity. Taking the frame as a site of activity will mean that the presence of the question of the object, in the shift from the static and the substantive to the actative, will demand to be taken as a different type of question and thus one demanding a different form of understanding. It will be with this demand that it will be possible, in the end, to return to the questions raised by the almost inescapable difficulty of writing on Ryman.

The link between work and the question of the object already plays a dominant role in the interpretation of modernism; what will be modernism's own self-reflective and self-defining activity. From Greenberg onwards the modern has always been linked to an active questioning of the status of the object. Indeed the recognition of this state of affairs serves as the basis of Yve-Alain Bois' dismissal of Ryman's interpretation of his own work:

> 'I approach printmaking in the same way that I approach painting, from the point of view of working with the basic possibilities of the medium,' says Ryman, modernist in spite of himself. Is there anyone who doesn't see that this way of speaking is no longer enough? that it is vacuous because it applies in various ways to everything of importance that modern art has ever produced? [2]

Bois' acute and often informative interpretation of Ryman locates his work at the limit if not at the end of modernism. (Bois' interpretation begins wisely by proclaiming the difficulty of offering any interpretation of Ryman and then goes on to utilise the reasons underpinning this identified difficulty as an essential part of his approach to Ryman.) The layered reflexivity that marks the modernist adventure becomes in Ryman, for Bois, excessive. The consequence of that 'excess' — an 'excess' (Bois' term) that arises precisely because of the depth of the work's reflexivity — is a 'failure'. It goes without saying, of course, that this is not the end envisaged by Ryman. For Bois this setup provides Ryman's work with its power. The work's 'failure' is its 'success':

> . . . every failure of his audacious attempt removes him further from his object, driving him to produce objects that are increasingly enigmatic and indeterminable. [3]

Bois' is an important interpretation of Ryman. It is also an interpretation that will become all the more significant because of its location of a disruptive potential within the detail of Ryman's work. Nonetheless the contention to be advanced here is that with certain works there is an identifiable strategy that resists any description in terms of the enigmatic. Moreover, the presence of any indeterminable elements would need to be located in relation to that which provided determination — namely the work of tradition — and therefore it would be precisely in terms of that relation that disruption can be relocated as an essential part of the work's own activity. Disruption will need a different setting. Consequently, at this stage, what must be taken up is the possibility of another interpretation of that activity within Ryman's project that Bois identifies as 'vacuous'. Rather than making the vacuity productive here the argument will be that instead of working strictly within the medium of painting, Ryman's own development can be presented as the investigation of the limit of a genre or medium (an investigation that nonetheless occurs within painting but in so doing causes what is meant by remaining 'within' painting to be recast). The exploration of the limit is occasioned by allowing the work of that medium — the medium's work hence the work's work — to explore from within it, within its own centre of activity, its relation to other artistic media. As has already been suggested, the specific activity occurring here is that the work of painting becomes an exploration of painting's relationship to sculpture. In part what this will mean is that the unity — the *reductio ad unam*, the unity of work and presentation — will itself have to be questioned. What must be examined, therefore, are the varying entailments given by that which is itself already presupposed in this attempted elimination of complexity. In general the reflexivity in question cannot be accepted as though its existence were unproblematic. Part of any reconsideration will mean that reflexivity will have to be approached in relation to what has already been identified as the logic of a part/apart. It will be in terms of this logic that the possibility of difference and thus a reworking of the medium will come to be formulated. Finally, the extent to which the works become, as Bois suggests, 'increasingly enigmatic and indeterminable' will also need to be taken up. What arises is the demand to return to the object. It will be a return that, in order to be pursued with the rigour demanded by Ryman's work, will necessitate another take on the possibility of pure objectivity. Here with Ryman's work, and even if the purity is in the end both miscast and misconstrued, this possibility is linked to the interplay, at least initially, of colour and form. Recognising that it will be in the conflicting attempts to define these terms, what is taken to be inherent in both purity and objectivity will come to be played out.

Tracing the taking up of the object, tracing, that is, the object's own concern with the question of the object where that concern comprises a fundamental part of the work's work — what has already been identified as the object-in-question — will involve a twofold move. On the one hand there is a detour through Kant. Rather than being simply circuitous, the necessity of that detour will be found in the possible connection between Kant's treatment of colour and form in the *Critique of Judgement* and the use and place of colour in Ryman's work. Colour's presence in his work could be described, again initially, in terms of that which is present as the turning and re-turning of white. On the other hand such a move will itself have to be constrained to take up the occurrence within the work of its own exploration (again an exploration that will form an essential part of the work's own work) of painting's relation to sculpture. Although these two elements will be treated equally, it will be essential to note that it is only in bringing them together that the full force of the becoming-object will emerge.

## Kant, Colour, Form

The link to Kant is already fraught with problems. Indeed why should there be a link if Ryman's work is itself situated, as has been argued, at the site of modernity's most intense self-reflection? The answer to that question lies in part with the work. In other words it is to be found in the detail of a number of paintings. Furthermore, Ryman's work will admit of interesting and important divisions.[4] There is, for example, despite the presence of white paint, an important difference between the Winsor paintings of the 1960s and a number of different white paintings of the same period as well as later. In, for example, works such as *Untitled* (1965), *Twin* (1966), *Surface Veil I* (1970), *Surface Veil II* (1970), *Surface Veil III* (1971), there is the presentation of the all-white field. Moreover, they involve the presentation of works which raise the question of the object in ways that are initially to be differentiated from works such as *Adelphi* (1967), *Surface Veil* (1970-1), *Range* (1983), *Access* (1983) and *Credential* (1985). Works such as *Monitor* (1978), for example, may provide a third category. What would be interesting about this third group is that it would question the rigidity of these distinctions or differentiations while maintaining them. The differentiations at play here are not temporal — pertaining to chronological time and thus to the work's dating; they are intended to mark minimal divisions in the way the works work. As such, of course, they will introduce the possibility of a different and more complex time. What is it, then, about the former group of works that allows recourse to Kant? The initial difficulty in answering this question is that the answer will pertain with equal force to other monochrome paintings and is therefore a general claim about a particular form of minimalism. The other major difficulty is that the possibility of establishing a link between beauty and the monochromatic will founder because of the failure of the monochromatic field to rid itself of the possibility of a founding complexity. As will be seen the beauty of 'pure colour' will prove impossible for similar reasons. The important point here will be that it is precisely this failure that reveals something about the nature of this form of minimalism.

As a way of proceeding it may be more appropriate to work back from Kant. Given that what is of fundamental importance is the relationship between colour and form and the way their interconnection yields the object, what will be central is Kant's discussion of colour in §14 of the *Critique of Judgement*.[5] This section is itself an 'elucidation' of the preceding one in which Kant has shown that 'pure judgements of taste' are those particular judgements 'on which charm and emotion have no influence'. It is worthwhile noting the other major aspect of §13. What is significant there is that, within it, the possibility of both the differentiation and the link between beauty and colour is established. Kant continues that the absence of charm and emotion means that what is identified as the 'pure judgement of taste' will have as 'its determining ground merely the purposiveness of the form'. Charm and emotion may be present but only insofar as they are connected to the 'satisfaction' arising from the beautiful. Nonetheless in terms of that which provides the judgement with its basis, it is 'purposiveness' and 'form' that play the pivotal role. What is meant by 'form' is clarified at the beginning of the *Critique of Pure Reason* in which sensation is distinguished from what allows appearances to be ordered. The latter is 'the form of appearance' (B34). It is worth noting how in the First Critique Kant continues this opening articulation of form since the division between experience and form will be just as important in the Third Critique. After having made his opening move Kant continues:

> That in which alone the sensations can be posited and ordered in a certain form, cannot itself be a sensation: and therefore while the matter of all appearance is given to us *a posteriori* only, its form must lie ready for the sensations *a priori* in the mind, and so must allow being considered apart from all sensation. (B34) [6]

What is immediately significant in this formulation is that the form of appearance is already present as part of the condition of appearance's possibility. The question in this instance however is how the precise relation between form and the 'purposiveness of form' already identified is to be understood. While beauty will pertain to the subject there must be an aspect of what is given to consciousness that allows for commensurability between subject and object (the latter understood as the taking over of that which is given).

As a beginning what must be recognised is that form, in the strictly Kantian sense, is not the formal quality of the object as such, it therefore should not be taken as an abstraction; in other words it cannot be understood as nothing other than the object's abstracted form. It is rather that form is both located and grounded in the nature of the difference between the *a priori* and the *a posteriori*. It is this site that is difficult. What can be drawn from a number of passages within the text is that what formally links the aesthetic and the moral is the question of form. The point that has to be made here is that form pertains to the universal quality that inheres in each instance (inheres in the experience of that which is experienced; maintaining this twofold is essential). Satisfaction is linked to the particular's opening up (and opening up to) universality. The satisfaction therefore involves that which is not yielded by sensation. It is the other quality. Aesthetical judgement is the judging of form.

Pursuing the question of form will mean taking up Kant's own examples. The automatic answer to the question of form will involve the distinction between that which presents itself — eg the tulip — and the way in which this instance will come to play a role in what is described in §57 as the 'purposive attuning of the imagination to agreement with the faculty of concepts in general'. It will be the recognition of the 'unconditioned purposiveness' both in beautiful art and in the beautiful in general which will have to involve the *a priori*. The automatic response to the question of form will involve therefore a twofold division. There may be, however, the possibility that this division may be obviated. Moreover, were it not for the *a priori* quality inherent in this formulation then the reciprocity between subject and object would generate and sustain the satisfaction in question. Indeed it is possible to go further and argue that it is only in terms of the *a priori* that it is possible to maintain the connection between the different faculties since what allows for the points of intersection is that which is present *a priori*. Utilising a formulation offered in §42 it is possible to suggest that the difficulty that will continue to emerge will involve accounting for the difference between what is described as 'the form of a practical maxim' and the actual practical maxim. The importance of the distinction is clear. Its significance lies in the fact that it is only by virtue of the form — and thus its necessarily *a priori* presence — that it is then possible to argue for the maxim's universal force and applicability. The ground of universality is the *a priori*.

In §14 colour is put forward as a way of furthering the elucidation between the beautiful and states necessarily linked to sensation such as charm, the pleasant etc. What will need to be noted is how colour (and musical tone) will figure in the beautiful and in the sensations pertaining to charm and the pleasant. Once again it will be the nature of the distinction that will be significant. What Kant describes as 'mere colour' — the green of green grass — is wrongly thought, by others, to be beautiful. The reason why such thoughts misconstrue the relationship between beauty and colour is because in these instances what works to provide the 'basis' of such a conclusion — the thought's determining ground — is 'the matter of representations'. This type of colour is necessarily linked to sensation. By virtue of its link to sensation, 'mere colour' cannot be identified as beautiful and, as such, can be no more than pleasant. However colour, and musical tone, have another possibility (what will emerge as the possibility of universality). They need not be reduced to the level of sensation. In this regard Kant remarks

> that the sensation of colours and of tone have a right to be regarded as beautiful only in so far as they are pure. This is a determination which concerns their form and is the only [element] of these representations which admits with certainty of universal communicability.[7]

Even though Kant links his discussion of colour to the theories of Euler, the general position that emerges is that colour can be taken as formal. After the allusion to Euler there comes a passage of considerable importance in which Kant clarifies what is meant by the description 'pure':

> . . . 'pure' in a simple mode of sensation means that its uniformity is troubled and interrupted by no foreign sensation, and it belongs merely to the form; because here we can abstract from the quality of that mode of sensation (abstract from the colours and tone, if any, which it represents). Hence *all simple colours, so far as they are pure, are regarded as beautiful*; composite colours have not this advantage because, as they are not simple, we have no standard for judging whether they should be called pure or not.[8] [My emphasis]

What should be added immediately here is Kant's further claim made a few paragraphs later that the 'purity of colour' will have the consequence of 'making the form more exactly, definitely and completely intuitable . . .'. To begin with, however, it must be recognised that there is far more involved here than would be yielded either by emphasising the process of abstraction or highlighting the supplementary role of colour. What needs to be held in place is the original claim that colour has 'the right to be regarded as beautiful' (leaving to one side for the moment the question of whether Kant was, even in his own terms, correct to make such a claim). The 'right' in question is of course inextricably bound up with purity. While the link to Ryman may appear to be slipping from view, what is essential to the white canvas, to the monochromatic space, is a purity in which the singularity of colour is absolutely coextensive with the singularity of form and thus, in its presentation, the purity of form will be linked to another take on the project of beautiful art. The importance of form, coupled with its ineliminable link to Kant, comprises an essential part of modernism.[9] Pursuing the Kantian connection — and in the end showing its own internal impossibility — will cause the works of modernism, the works identified within that field, to be reopened and thus able to be reworked. It will be in terms of the interplay of opening and work that another interpretation will be possible. It is in this sense that Kant's work cannot be avoided. It provides the possibility of thinking autonomy.

For Kant colour can be a sensation insofar as it is linked to the pleasant. (Tracing the detail of this claim would necessitate taking up the distinction established by Kant in §3 between 'objective sensation' and 'subjective sensation'.) Nonetheless, the distinction between on the one hand what is beautiful and that which is either charming or pleasant on the other is not a distinction of degree. This is the fundamental point of departure. In the passage under consideration purity is located 'in a simple mode of sensation'. It is located with the sensation even though it cannot be reduced to the sensation itself. Within the sensation what is meant by purity is that what is present as pure exists such that it is not itself mediated by another conflicting sensation. The reason why this is the case is that purity is neither supplementary, nor is it there as an addition to form. It belongs to the form itself; and, in this sense, it is formal. After making this point Kant then adds that this occurs 'because we abstract from the quality of that mode of sensation'. What is being suggested here is that the purity of colour can in some sense be taken out of a range of colours. The process of abstraction would be the identification of purity. Abstraction, or perhaps the process of abstraction, needs to be approached with caution. Time is vital in order to explain what is involved in the movement of abstraction.

Abstraction in this instance is neither a drawing out nor is it a simply retroactive attribution. Beauty is not identified as only existing after the event. The abstraction, or rather the process of abstraction, would aim at uncovering that which was originally pure. In other words it would uncover what was already present. In this move there is a necessary differentiation from the temporality of sensation. Composite colours — colours which are the result of combination — cannot be regarded as beautiful. However the explanation given in the passage is initially unsatisfactory. Kant argues that the reason for not describing them as beautiful is that there is no 'standard for judging'. There exists nothing in terms of which composite colours could be deemed beautiful or not. They could not, therefore, be described as pure. What, however, does this mean? What is absent from these concerns?

*Robert Ryman,* Adelphi, *1967, oil on linen with wax paper frame, 259x259cm, and* Surface Veil II, *1970, oil on linen, 366x366cm (above);* Surface Veil III, *1971, oil on cotton, 366x366cm, and* Range, *1983, oil and enamelac on fibreglass with aluminium fasteners, 131x120cm (below) (reproduced courtesy of Pace Wildenstein, New York)*

While the straightforward answer is that the absence in question refers to the requisite links necessary to establish universality, this needs to be understood in terms of the conditions for universality itself. As has already been noted, it is only with the *a priori* that universality will be possible. Composite colours are not pure because they are both contingent as well as being an addition. (Addition needs to be given a precise location. Here addition will always mean in addition to the 'purposiveness of form'.) As such they could not form the basis of a 'pure judgement of taste'. Purity of colour, however, because it relates to form and thereby already pertains to the ground of universality, can be beautiful. Purity of colour could almost be described as the exemplary instance of form. Unlike the tulip (cf §18) it does not have to be held apart from other possibilities. While the tulip could be the object of different and incompatible judgements, the purity of colour (whiteness for example) existing in and of itself, has neither a link to 'design' nor is there the effective presence of a 'definite purpose'. This possibility for the purity of colour — a possibility not pursued by Kant — needs to be situated in relation to the formulation of beauty offered at the end of §17. In that instance beauty is importantly linked to form:

> Beauty is the *form of the purposiveness of an object*, so far as this is received in it without any representation of a purpose.[10] [My emphasis]

In order to explain this formulation Kant offers an explanatory note, and in this note the example of the 'tulip' is given. After comparing a 'work of art' with the tulip he goes on to conclude, in relation to the latter, that a tulip, as with flowers in general, is 'regarded as beautiful, because in perceiving it we find a certain purposiveness which, in our judgement, is preferred to no purpose at all'. The tulip lends itself to this possibility. It does, of course, also lend itself to other descriptions and thus to other judgements. In his Introduction Kant has already located the activity of the subject as always engaging with the 'same territory of experience'. (It is not as though the world is different for each judgement. It is rather that difference is defined by the nature of the world of each judgement.) Within that 'territory' the tulip has a number of possibilities. It can be the object of different judgements. The judgement of taste precludes logical judgement — the presence and absence of concepts works to define the nature of the judgement in each case — and yet, in relation to the tulip, such judgements are possible. Purpose can always be reintroduced by changing the type of judgement.[11] Leaving aside the viability of the distinction between types of judgement and thus of being able to maintain their complete differentiation, what has to be taken up is the question of whether pure colour has the same status as that attributed to the flower. The question can be made more specific by addressing the nature of the relation between whiteness (understood as the purity of the colour white) and the tulip. It should be clear, however, that in both instances what will be involved is the representation of the object to the subject. At no time is there the suggestion that beauty is a formal criterion of the object *per se*. Beauty will always have to be located in the subject/object relation and therefore in terms of that which facilitates and maintains the relation.

The basis of an answer to the question of the connection (or failure of connection) between whiteness and the tulip has already been suggested. In the case of the tulip it provides the locus for different judgements. The question therefore is quite simple: is this the case with the purity of colour? In other words, is it the case with whiteness? In answering, the possibility of taking up the viability of Kant's own argument needs to be considered. It may be that the difficulty with the question of colour may stem from a confusion in Kant's own formulation. There may have been a conflation of aesthetic form with objective form. Were this to have been Kant's undertaking then not only would this have denied the singularity of the aesthetic judgement thereby rendering otiose both the ground and the necessity for the aesthetic judgement, it would also have made form no more than a quality of the object. What this latter point would have demanded is a concept to sustain the universality of the object's quality, while at the same time it would have denied the ineliminable role that the anthropological plays in the formulation of the aesthetic.

It should not be thought that it is impossible to draw this type of conclusion from §14. The problem with it however is that it misses the precise possibility that is also missed by Kant. What is at stake here is in fact exemplarity itself. If beauty pertains to the relationship between the subject and the representation of the object in which that relation is taken to be a harmony between the subject and that which is given to it, then with the tulip what allows for harmonic accord is that which inheres *a priori* (or which is present *a priori*) within it. This is a quality that is given by the sensation; and, in being given it must also be separated from that in which it is given. The latter element is of course the sensation. With the purity of colour another type of relation will pertain. In this instance it is not as though beauty has become more than a quality of the object — something else is involved. What must be pursued, therefore, is the extent to which it depends upon the sensation in which it is given. Pure colour existing in and for itself in its representation to the subject does not necessitate (or at the very least is implicitly presented in the text as not necessitating) the complex presence of association and disassociation signalled above. What this means here is that what would be given as beautiful would not have the same setup as the tulip. In that case the *a priori* was there with the form of the purposiveness of the object present without the presence of purpose. The latter element, namely the absence of any representation of purpose, was not to be perceived. In the case of pure colour — whiteness — this is not a possibility. There is no purpose as such. This is the reason why firstly it would seem to be a paradigmatic instance of the beautiful and why secondly it is not a question of the conflation of aesthetic and objective form. And yet of course it is the actual impossibility of the former — pure beauty — that will open the path to Ryman. The impossibility will lie in the problem of presentation.

Colour is beautiful to the extent that what is presented is the purity of form. With whiteness — or any other pure, ie non-composite colour — there is an envisaged separation. Form is all that is present. Form here figures within the distinction between pure and composite colours. As has already been suggested, understanding this distinction turns around the figure of time. What time means in this instance is inextricably linked to the presentation and with it the formulation of form. Purity and simplicity have to be presented as such. Mediation would not only introduce the addition or alteration (the actual changes would need to be specified), it would also undermine the possibility of an initial and already present universality. The universality of form lies in its *a priori* status. With colour — beautiful colour — there is only form. Pure colour involves a twofold disassociation. In the first place, it is disassociated from composite colour; in the second, it is to be disassociated from that which may bear two particular and necessarily different types of judgement, eg the tulip. The force of these disassociations is to be found in what they yield. Here it is a temporal division between a secondary site of judgement in which the *a priori* and the *a posteriori* are both present, even though it is the *a priori* quality that is linked necessarily to universality and which is communicated or communicates itself, and a singular present that has no more than this *a priori* quality in the strict sense that all that is present is form itself. (This is, after all, the description of 'pure' offered in §14.)

What is being suggested here is that with the 'pure' and in the place of a complex setup that involves the copresence of two particular aspects of an object, there is an original purity. What characterises this founding purity is that what is present has no more than an *a priori* quality. And yet if this description is accurate how could pure colour ever present itself? In a very intriguing passage towards the end of §14 Kant, in attempting to elucidate the 'form of an object of sense', seems to suggest that form amounts to the object's formal qualities — even though this formulation is turned such that these properties become that which makes the judgement possible; and yet, having made this claim, he then seems to complicate his position by arguing that:

> To say that the purity of colours and tones, or their variety and contrast, seem to add to beauty does not mean that they supply a homogeneous addition to our satisfaction in the form because they are pleasant in themselves; but they do so because *they make the form more exactly, definitely, and completely intuitable*, and besides, by their charm [excite the representation, while they] awaken and fix our attention on the object itself.[12] [My emphasis]

What becomes complicated here is that 'purity of colour', for example, adds to the intuition of form. More than that, the presence of colours means that they have the potential to charm and thus to hold the observer's eye. The object's presence becomes more emphatic because of the effective presence of the purity of colour. What is involved is an 'object of sense'. Colour is linked directly to sense. In being thus linked, what it enables is a state of affairs in which it can become ' . . . more exactly, definitely and completely intuitable'. It would be absurd to allow for the possibility that form could ever be recognised in any other way. The intuition of form takes place at one and the same time. With regard to the purity of colour existing in itself and thus being presented in itself, it is necessarily other than that which is linked to sense; moreover, to the extent that it can exist in itself, it must be able to be intuited 'exactly, definitely and completely'. Again, what returns is the question of how the purity of colour is able to be present such that, in its being present, it escapes from being regarded as a sensation and therefore as that which attracts attention to the object. Is the purely *a priori* a coherent possibility?

It is as though the same question keeps returning. The difficulty with avoiding the question lies in the fact that it arises from what is fundamental to Kant's formulation, namely an unequivocal distinction between purity and the composite; a distinction in which the former has the quality of a given and founding purity and simplicity, and the second a necessarily mediated presence. The nature of the distinction is such that, in being presented in terms of the opposition between the *a priori* and the *a posteriori*, it must allow for the presentation of that which has the quality of being and thus existing *a priori*. It must further be the case that it is this purity — pure form — which must be able to be experienced as such. And yet it cannot be experienced as such; it must always be identified by an act of demarcation. Even in the case of pure colour in which there is no question of other possible judgements, there still needs to be an accompanying cognitive activity that differentiates the pure from the composite. Pure colour could not give itself except in so far as it is recognised and thus experienced in an act of differentiation. Its purity resides in part in its being able to be separated from other possibilities. What will endure, therefore, is the inscription of differentiation and of the process of establishing and maintaining the purity of form as pure. Furthermore it is the singular *a priori* that always comes to be mediated, thereby casting doubt on the possibility of singularity. Here, more significantly, because the only possibility for the singularity of form was provided by the *a priori*, its impossibility has the twofold effect of putting the distinction between the *a priori* and the *a posteriori* into question at the same time as reopening, as a question, the possibility of the singular. What will emerge is that it is the conclusion drawn from Kant that will play a vital role in taking up the work of Ryman. What emerges from the attempt to establish a founding singularity — the singularity of form present *a priori*, present almost independently of sensation — is that what comes to be affirmed in its place is a founding and irreducible complexity; this state of affairs can be designated as the problem of form. With Ryman's work, therefore, while there is the temptation of attempting to enact the singularity of form, or perhaps more accurately to see and interpret the work in that light, there is an integral part of his work that resists such a reduction. More significantly, here, it resists it as an essential part of the work's work.

Prior to taking up Ryman's works the problem of form needs to be rearticulated. What has emerged is that colour could be beautiful if it were pure. Purity is the presence of form. Beauty, if it is present, must communicate itself universally and it must be universally communicable. The basis of universality — its ground — is the *a priori*. While the possibility of a pure colour is marked by the process that holds it apart from its being presented, it must at the same time be part of what is presented. Consequently, while its absolute purity is impossible — the traces and marks of differentiation and division will always intrude into the process of differentiation — what the impossibility signals is not the impossibility of singularity but rather the recognition that singularity will always be an after-effect of a founding complexity. It emerges out of an initial irreducible setup; and, here, irreducibility must be understood as anoriginally present. Impossibility, therefore, will have escaped the determinations of the *via negativa* by affirming an-other presence.

## Painting Lines

Impossibility having emerged as the affirmation of anoriginal complexity rather than existing as an end in itself becomes, here, the means by which to take up the work of Ryman's paintings. Two elements of the proper name need to be identified in advance. The first is that it names, as has been suggested, an important division between different strategies and procedures within painting. Secondly, it names the presence of works which complicate these divisions even though they work, at the same time, to maintain them. What is essential, therefore, is to show the ineliminable complexity that is already at work in the proper name (a complexity, in sum, that the name names). Two paintings with which it becomes possible to start are *Winsor 34* (1966) and *Twin* (1966). Perhaps the dominant interpretive frame — the frame given by modernism after Kant — that has been taken to these works is well summed up in Naomi Spector's comment that in them

> . . . the work was about the nature of paint: the paint was the content of the paintings, as well as the form. They had no meaning outside the paint and the supporting material and the history of the process of application.[13]

It is not difficult to see in this interpretation the conception of modernism that comes from Kant — the evocation of the purity of form — whose contemporary formulation is given in the writings of Greenberg.[14] It is present here in the posited coextensivity of form and content. While advocates of purity, a position held for slightly different reasons by both Greenberg and Rosenberg, may have elided the distinction found in Kant between the *a priori* and *a posteriori,* this elision does not alter the fact, as has emerged, that the Kantian basis of the distinction is itself untenable. Once again, and despite this elision, the contemporary adoption or even adaptation of purity is therefore equally problematic. What remains unthought and therefore unacknowledged in such interpretive work is the question of complexity. The recognition of this state of affairs — a recognition that will allow complexity — will have the direct consequence of freeing these works from an already determined position, and therefore from their having to form part of the history that has been created for them and within which they function as that history's creations. This opening, while always allowing for other interpretive possibilities, will need to be traced in the works themselves. It is not just there.

Part of the force of the description of *Winsor 34* that is present in Spector's formulation is that it does seem to capture an essential quality of the work. The limiting of the work — perhaps even the delimiting of the work's work — to the operation of paint creates a necessary internality that establishes almost by definition the work's autonomy. Furthermore the attempted elimination of any clear distinction between form and content not only reinforces the work's autonomy, albeit negatively by the denial of the effective presence of either representation or mimesis, but it is as though the work gives itself — it creates the setting of a founding purity. What needs to be argued in contradistinction to these positions — the argument for and from the anoriginal presence of productive complexity — is that the singular use of paint, far from denying the distinction between form and content, actually redefines it and, in that movement, the nature of both the distinction and singularity are themselves repositioned. In addition, the attempt to deny other possible sites of meaning — sites other than paint — is already sundered by including 'the history of the process of application' as part of the site. (It is as though the interplay of apart/a part signals the primordiality of relation.) Spector's interpretation is by no means unique in the claims that it makes. They are claims, as has been suggested, that accord with dominant elements in the construction of modernism. Tracing the impossibility of the purity of form in Kant is at the same time to have traced the impossibility of the formulations provided in Spector's position. What then of the painting? The importance of this question is obvious. It is the work, and therefore the interpretive movement that concerns itself with the work's work, that must be the point of focus.

*Winsor 34* forms part of a number of paintings all of which derive their names from the source of the paint used. This particular work was created by a cumulative addition of strokes each using up the totality of paint on the brush. In the end the effect was the presentation of brushwork. How then is this work to be understood? There are two initial responses to this question. The first concerns the intentionality to be attributed to the work; the work's own self-appointed project; in sum, its intentional logic.[15] The second pertains to the site of interpretation. With regard to the work's intention it will always be possible to argue that the use of a single colour and the restriction of work to the presentation of brush strokes intends to create a closed world of work. The closure, here another term for autonomy, is the closing off of the framed from the intrusion of any outside element, with it the framed then becomes enclosed as a self-contained inside. The setting for such an interpretation would be the adoption of that interpretive frame that sanctioned, allowed and thus necessitated this autonomy. A fundamental part of this setup would be the positing of an initial and founding simplicity. These two components are interrelated; between them there exists a sustaining reciprocity. What other possibility would there be? What other takes are there? In responding to these questions what must be maintained is intentional logic. The virtue of retaining this formulation is that it will allow for the following initial judgement. If the intentional logic is as described above, then it can be shown to have come undone in its effectuation. If it is not then it allows for another quality to be attributed to the work. Either way what will emerge is a construal of the work that resists the already present determinations of autonomy and thus of a posited and initial purity (purity understood as that coextensivity of form and content that would be untroubled even by the presence of different colours). It is this latter point that will need to be shown.

Paint, the white paint that creates the work, in its application creates lines. In their progressive construction the lines of paint, white paint, create within them the setting for/ of other lines. (What must continue to be recognised is that this identification of the progressive construction of lines has greater significance in terms of its inherent temporality than that which would be given by its clear spatial determinations. Time will have priority over space.) These other lines refer to this setting — the setting in place of lines — while at the same time referring to what could be described as a more generalised setting of paint. This is what Spector means by the 'history of application'. There is therefore a double reference; a double setting. It will be necessary to return to this site of doubling. At this stage, however, what must be obtained is a setting in which the interplay of form and content, an interplay the position of which is provided by the nature of the lines, can be taken up. The centrality of the line, and thus the need to reinterpret the line's presence, will also emerge as a fundamental part of the interpretation undertaken here of Pollock and Kiefer. It is as though the reinterpreted line is the beginning of an-other take on painting. The setup that must be pursued therefore pertains to the relationship between on the one hand, the double setting of line and paint and, on the other, the way in which the form/content distinction is present. As will be suggested it is the double setting that reworks the form/content distinction and consequently will work to place it beyond its already given place. In other words it is not as though the attempt to show that the posited coextensivity between form and content is marked by a necessary impossibility which returns the distinction as though it were untouched. There can be neither a simple nor a straightforward return. The interpretive activity that overcomes the posited coextensivity of form and content will yield an-other possibility for the distinction. Its presence will mark out complexity. Pursuing the distinction has consequences therefore that fall beyond the domain created by simple prediction. What must be taken into consideration is the effect of the temporality of interpretation.

As has already been indicated, one way of understanding the proposed coextensivity of form and content is in terms of the consequent absence, within the frame, of any representational or mimetic content. With such a possibility the work would be self-defined, and by virtue of that type of definition, necessarily self-referential. It would enclose and consequently would have become closed in upon itself. With this closure, with what will have emerged in the end as a putative closure, the frame has become the site of a conjectured pure internality. Such a world need not have only one appearance. Within this internal world a form of invention can be maintained, insofar as the work of paint can take on different modes of presentation. Brushwork can have varying forms of presence. (This would be the conventional way of distinguishing between, for example, *Winsor 34* and *Twin* while maintaining their overall identity.) What is essential in order that pure internality be held in place is that the paintwork neither represents nor presents mimetically that which takes place outside. The outside must be positioned and fixed outside, thus positioning and fixing the outside *as* outside; the reciprocity here needs to be acknowledged. Before seeking to show that such a possibility fails two things need to be noted. The first involves reiterating the point that such a description seems to accord with the work. The second is that what is under discussion here is not the work's meaning where meaning is taken as an end in itself. With regard to the first of these points, what it indicates is the extent to which the reception of these works has created a setup in which the works almost 'naturally' embody the original language of reception. The problem here is that not only is such a setting far from natural, it also precludes consideration being given to what occurs in the constitution of the object as an object of interpretation; the actual process of constitution. With regard to the second, what needs to be maintained is the interplay between ontology and signification. Once ontology — here the being proper to art work, object as work — is repositioned away from the substantive and towards the actative, such a move will almost necessarily upset the possibility of any easy separation of work and meaning.

Returning to the work in question the implausibility of its functioning as pure internality is itself given in Spector's description. The point that has to be made is that it is the work that works against the description, if the description is taken as a whole. She identifies the coextensivity of form and content while allowing the painting to bear, with regard to the work's meaning, the 'history of the application' of paint. It is this twofold that has already been identified in terms of a double setting. In the first place there is the setting in place of line; in the second there is the inscription of the history of paint's application. With the lines in this work there is the possibility of seeing in their juxtaposition — a serial juxtaposition that works with and within a certain repetition — a complex time. Moreover the complexity of this time will, in part, have been given by the history of paint's 'application', ie by the history of painting. The question, however, is one of how the determinations within that history are to be presented. Given determinations merely repeat what is already there; other possibilities therefore need different openings. This accounts for why, here, instead of taking the predetermined conception of the minimal and the monochromatic as given, they will come to be reworked; it will be in this reworking that the presence of the object as becoming-object is able to emerge. Part of the project of reworking will be time. Indeed, the distinction between either abstraction or minimalism and painting that from within the conventions governing these earlier forms is taken as either representational or mimetic, is time. The difference does not lie in the content *tout court*. Moreover, allowing the difference to be thought of in terms of time indicates further why the Kantian formulation of an initial and founding simplicity cannot work. With Kant, and indeed with the convention of minimalism, what was given was to be presented as simultaneous with itself. It is given at one and the same time. The purity of the object would have been sundered once it has to be given again; the reduction of the object to the pure expression of objectivity comes undone once repetition is no longer articulated within the Same. One gift will work to mediate the other. The instant must be maintained insofar as it is the temporal correlate to purity. Time will be the undoing of the instant if the instant is taken to be the original and primary state.

And yet while it may be that the minimal needs to be given at one and the same time if the ontologico-temporal setup proper to purity is to be maintained, it is in fact representational painting that actually intends to fulfil this demand. Indeed, if it is possible to generalise then it can be argued that, operating within its own conventions, representation has to fulfil such a demand. With regard to representational painting what is given is the totality of narrative; the displayed content. This will be, in part, the reason why modes of entry — eg, the focal point — will be essential to uncovering and determining the painting's meaning. Entry should resist the possibility of equivocation since it will be the way into the work that lays its content before the viewing eye. The detail therefore will be what is given in addition. It will supplement what has already been presented and which is already present. While it may be that within interpretation the specific nature of the detail may, in the end, unsettle or put into question both the unity and the semantic security of the initial presentation, it remains the case that what is given is, from the start, a unified narrative. The time of representation involves a single presentation. It is thus that there is an important analogy between representational painting and the image. Both are projected at one and the same time. While this may set up a series of expectations that cannot be fulfilled, what endures as envisaged is that temporal simultaneity figures in each of them. It is this temporal structure that is absent from the work of *Winsor 34*, and it will also be absent from the other works identified as belonging to the same group, *Untitled* (1965), *Twin* (1965), *Surface Veil I* (1970), *Surface Veil II* (1970) and *Surface Veil III* (1971). The problem of any grouping has to be acknowledged from the start and yet there is a quality that will allow these works to be taken up together.

The quality is the brushwork. While it will always be necessary to return to specific works to trace the effectuation of this work, what seems to characterise a number of Ryman's paintings is the particular way this quality is present. Perhaps it should be added that its being present in the work of Ryman does not preclude its presence elsewhere in other works linked to other names. Problems only arise in this domain if the proper name rather than the specificity of work is taken as limiting the work's scope and range. As a beginning it is necessary to start with a negative description. The reason for this negativity is not because the work functions as a negation of other possibilities — such a possibility would be too straightforward and thus too mechanistic if it were thought to be all that was involved — but that part of the work's work will be a disassociation or differentiation that marks out the presence of a division which will come to be connected. This is the logic of the apart/a part. There is a certain irony here since, it could be argued, it is precisely this logic whose work has already been identified by Spector in her having to claim — a claim that would otherwise be simply contradictory — that the work is at the same time pure internality while bearing the traces of the history of paint's application; in other words bearing within the frame the presence of that which was necessarily external to it and thus excluded from it.

The negative description is twofold. On the one hand what is taking place with these works is not reducible to the temporality of the instant nor, on the other, is it expressible in terms of a simultaneity of field and therefore of a singular or unified content. It is clear that there is a necessary reciprocity between these two elements. And yet of course it would appear that if the frame were to have been taken as yielding pure colour then there would have been the presentation, at the instant, of purity. The impossibility of purity and with it the retention of the instant as parasitic upon a more complex time — a complexity already present — has already emerged from taking up the possibility of purity in Kant. Here, what must be shown is why simultaneity is not possible and how that impossibility will be linked to an affirmative project. It should be added that to the extent that there cannot be pure negation, equally there cannot be pure affirmation. From within the ambit of interpretation both negation and affirmation, in being held together at the same time, need to be taken as signalling the primordiality of relation.

With these works, with the setting in place of lines, the brush moves — has moved — across the canvas providing the paint and inscribing brushwork. The brush having moved is lifted, once again it is covered in paint and the brush is then reapplied to the surface. Once more the paint is applied. Once again the brush strokes bear the mark of the application. Again the brush is lifted, and again the paint comes to be applied. Again it is applied until the paint gives way. There is a necessity at work in this description. It is present with the repeated use of the word 'again'. There can be no real description that does not demand the use of this word. In *Winsor 34* what is occurring seems to involve a repetition. A work that enacts its being enacted again. The question that must be addressed is: what is it that is marked out by the retention and repetition of the word 'again'? What is happening 'again'? The straightforward answer is: the application of paint. While such a response is accurate, what it leaves out of consideration is that the application of paint is the painting's work. Recognising the link between application and work, however, does not involve positing the coextensivity of form and content. There are two reasons why this is the case. The first is that arguing for an immediate link between form and content is a semantic claim about the work's meaning. In this example it is what would amount to the claim that the meaning of the work is its presence on the canvas; the work is about itself. The second and related point is that it would still the work of time. Time, understood as the movement of the becoming-object, would have to have been stilled — the transformation of the actative into the substantive — since a precondition for the possibility of the conflating interpretation would be an insistence on the work being taken as already over and complete. Rather than concentrating on the effectuation of the work, the work as that which is at work, it would position work as the instantiation of the coextensivity of form and content. In other words it would involve its presentation in terms of both the temporality of the instant and its related ontology. The force of the 'again' would be undone. Once 'again' is given a determination where it is taken as signalling the continuity of movement, the continual movement of enacting (moreover, as shall be suggested, it will be a continuity that precludes synthesis), then what is retained as central is the continuity of becoming and with it the continuity of the becoming-object. Part of this process will lead to a questioning of frames and borders. In this instance it will be a questioning stemming from the object and therefore from allowing the object's mode of being to be central.

These points can be pursued in *Surface Veil I*. In this instance the 'again' has to do with the presence of brushwork. Here it involves the relationship between the horizontal and the vertical. And yet the relation is not just spatial. It is of course spatial to the extent that its place can be plotted and defined as taking place at a particular place on the canvas. However, a description of the work that took the form of a spatial semiotic would leave out, almost necessarily, a fundamental part of the work. An interpretive move of this type could not track the way in which a synthetic unity — a unity gestured at the by the all-white colour of the canvas — is precluded by the work's work. Indeed it is possible to go further and argue that the very fact that the work is wholly white compounds the inscription of a temporal difference. The reason why it is essential to insist on time here is that the division involves a separation in the application of paint. It is a separation that cannot be bridged or brought together. It is not as if it were simply two separate, though similar, marks that had been placed on the canvas at purportedly different moments in chronological time. Such marks — in terms of their specificity — might have been placed on the canvas at the same time. Here, because the nature of the brushwork resists assimilation or synthesis, there will be a different determination of time within this work. The time at work in the application of these postulated different marks is an irrelevance insofar as their interpretation is concerned. They do not mark out the work of time.

In the case of *Surface Veil I*, as in the case of *Winsor 34*, the application of paint has not just taken place at different moments in chronological time. The process that allowed what is present on the canvas to be present necessitates a holding apart in which each element functions as a setting for the other. The setting of one apart from others inscribes into the canvas, as its work, a sustained differentiation and connection that, taken together, comprises the work's work; taken together — a together that will always be apart — what is at work is the becoming-object. Becoming is both ontological and temporal; the becoming-object is therefore already timed. The interplay between what is presented within this complex interconnection needs to be taken beyond the forced and enforcing distinction of form and content. The repetition marked by the again within *Winsor 34* introduces a staging and thus a repetitive difference where the difference involves different temporal moments as well as spatial positions. Form and content, therefore, if they are to be retained as terms within which to describe the work of these paintings, will need to be given a temporal and spatial register. As a consequence they would lose their purely descriptive and semantic content by having been implicated in the centrality of work; once more the actative displacing the centrality of the substantive. The nature of brushwork within these paintings therefore can be taken as affirming a complexity that is anoriginal in that it is irreducible. The nature of their work works towards that which resists the synthesis and purity which is demanded by form and presupposed by narrative; this occurs not by these works merely enacting their negation but by their offering an-other possibility. This other possibility is, in part, what they are. In *Surface Veil I* the tension of a synthesis offered by colour but denied by work, once reworked becomes the work's productive force. Its presence sustains the work such that with the release of the negative — the abeyance of the *via negativa* — the founding complexity is given as present.

While *Twin* is the work that seems to come closest to the purity of form and in so doing to rehearse the definition of autonomy as the extrusion of any mimetic or representational content, the contrary is the case. What emerges is that the application of paint, rather than constructing a unified field, breaks that possibility by leaving the differing marks of application on the canvas as its — the work's — work. Again this is not the obvious point that paint is applied at different moments. The application of paint at varying stages — differing moments in the work's completion — will, for the most part, have been effaced by the differing applications having been integrated into the formation of a whole; the construction of a synthetic work. Here, with this work, this is not the case. In fact, as has been suggested, the possibility that this might be true because of the use of a single colour is in fact undone by the use of a single colour. It is the monochromatic painting which can sunder the expectations and projections of unity and synthesis only because it is monochromatic. The differing applications of paint that create *Twin* are present in terms of a serial repetition that affirms irreducibility by precluding synthesis. In terms of what could there be a synthesis? The only answer to this question is colour. And yet it is the actual way in which the colour — the singular colour — is applied that forestalls this possibility by allowing for a continuity of addition in which the relation between each addition is temporal insofar as the placing of paint has a constituting retroactive effect on earlier lines. There is not just the repetition of same. The movement within the work creates a tension that defies a simply spatial description by maintaining the dynamic presence of the double setting.

Finally, therefore, even though there will be important differences in the detailed description of *Surface Veil I*, *Surface Veil II*, and *Surface Veil III*, insofar as brushwork will always involve a regional specificity what is emerging is that, in terms of the ontological and temporal determinations introduced and sustained by brushwork in the paintings — the same will be true for *Winsor 34* and *Twin* — there is, nonetheless, an identifiable level of generality. The generality involves time and the way in which time allows for an already present and productive irreducibility within the canvas — present as the object of interpretation — which causes the object to present itself within a continuity and as a continuity, comprising the becoming-object. Complexity is not the site in which a posited purity has shown itself to be tainted by an ineliminable impurity. It is rather that complexity is the site of anoriginal difference in which the singular — here most markedly present in terms of colour — works, as an after-effect, to maintain the presence of complexity. Misconstruing the object — in, for example, the failure to recognise that the ineliminable link between meaning and ontology ties meaning into the work's work — would allow for the singular to be given interpretive and temporal priority. This would be the impossible move that advocated either a founding purity or an initial coextensivity of form and content. Here, however, there has been an-other possibility for colour.

### Painting Sculptures

With *Adelphi* something else has come into play. It is a possibility that is rehearsed throughout some of the work dating from 1967. Chronology here can be taken as marking that place at which space comes to play a constitutive role in painting. And yet if this description has any viability there is a question that will have to be addressed. If space is the preoccupation of sculpture, what is the role to be played by space in these paintings? The first thing to note is that it is not painted space; the internal representation of space. This is an-other space. Tracing the work of this use of space — spacing as an integral part of painting's work — will involve the presence of the logic of the apart/a part. This time, however, the logic is present in connection with painting's exploration of its relation to sculpture; an exploration that takes place within and as painting. It will be because of the constitutive presence of the exploration — an undertaking that is once again descriptive of the work's work — that it becomes possible to see in what way what is being maintained by work is what has been identified thus far as the object-in-question. It is maintained of course by the continuity of work and thus by the continuity of the becoming-object.

With *Adelphi* and *Surface Veil* (1970-1) there is an external element which has come to form part of the work. The element in question concerns how the work is attached to the wall. In general both the frame and the method by which the work is hung are considered irrelevant to the activity of painting. They add nothing as they are external to the work. While the activity of framing understood as a process within painting can be of central concern, the physical presence of the painting is usually taken to be that which is given within the frame. Even in those circumstances where there may be no actual physical frame as such, there is still the assumption of a frame insofar as the work is deemed to have ended — and thus to be no longer at work — at the painting's edge. Of the many ways to interpret this particular aspect of painting perhaps the most germane for these circumstances is furnished by space. The spacing that is proper to painting involves the internality of the work. Sculpture, on the other hand, involves a more literal space. In contrast to painting, sculpture works both within space and with the creation of space; spacing is relational. Sculpture involves an enacted spacing that occurs, physically, outside of itself. *Adelphi* and *Surface Veil* are not sculpture; and yet neither are they automatically and unequivocally painting. It is this complex setup, therefore, that needs to be pursued.

Both of these works consist of the application of paint to one surface (canvas, fibreglass) which is then attached to a further surface (wax paper) which is in turn attached to the wall with masking tape. The application of paint was only to the canvas or the fibreglass. The work was always more than the literal site of painting while the painting — the object designated as the painting — was always more than the application of paint. The question that insists is the question of the object: in what sense is what is taking place here a painting? The difficulty in responding to this question is that in order to describe the way in which these works operate, it is essential to note the build-up of surfaces, not just with the place of one surface on another, but with the way in which the presence of the masking tape must work to elevate the smooth contour of an edge which ends the site of painting. The inclusion of the tape means that because it plays a significant role in the formation of the object, it must play one in the object's interpretation. What is at work with the eruption of surfaces — an eruption taking place outside of a simple sequential development of surfaces — is the presence of a spacing more physical in nature than that which is internal to the constitutive work of painting. Interpreting physical presence will mean linking it to the creation of a spacing that is closer to sculpture than to painting.

With all of the works under consideration here — and the ones named are only a selection from a much larger range — there is a quality that links them. The quality is spacing. It should not be thought that brushwork is no longer a consideration. A detailed description of the ways in which these works work would necessitate recourse to brushwork. In this instance, however, what is of central importance is what is happening to the formation of the object. Consequently, changes that occur on the level of the object's physical appearance, once those changes are understood as involving the object of interpretation, will then demand a more complex description. Here, however, the spacing in question is contingent on the works occupying a specific place. Indeed, their capacity to take up spacing demands this place. The place in question is the wall. It is only because these works are hung, and therefore occupy the place of painting, that it is possible for them, in having been placed as paintings, to raise the question of sculpture. With *Adelphi* and *Surface Veil*, the sculptural possibilities are linked to the layering of the surface and thus the absence of a determining frame. In the case of *Range* and *Access* these possibilities inhere in the raising of panels or the use of elaborate bolts to fix the work to the wall in which the bolts, as with the masking tape, form a fundamental part of the work. With *Credential* the raising of the sculptural resides in the incorporation of a projected surface that creates different surfaces within and as the work.

With the detail of these works what emerges is an intrusion into space and thus a positioning that spaces; it is one in which the possibility of the object having become sculpture is, however, not an option. They work within the possibility of the sculptural while remaining distanced from it. The condition that allows for this link to sculpture is their presence as paintings. What this means is that, to the extent that they form part of the possibility of sculpture, they remain apart from it. Equally, to the extent that these works endure as painting and thus form part of the domain of painting, their incorporation of spacing into their work means that they are, at the same time, apart from painting. These works therefore operate in terms of the logic of the apart/a part. Moreover, as painting is the precondition for the investigation, from within painting, of painting's relation to the sculptural and with it to the externality of spacing, painting and sculpture could not function as the negation of each other. The absence of negation is also signalled by the necessity of the apart/a part to operate at the same time. What this copresence indicates is, once again, the effective presence of an irreducible origin.

What arises with painting's attempt to explore, as painting, its own relation to sculpture, where that undertaking is not a contingent possibility but an essential part of the work's work, is that the details of the works in question can be given meanings that are then able to be integrated into the nature of the work. The interpretation of the bolts in *Access*, for example, rather than being indicative of either a simple or self-reflexive concern with objectivity, will be able to be taken as an instance of a more sustained questioning of the activity of painting. It is more sustained because it comes from outside of painting, even though the outside is incorporated within the painting itself. Here there is the possibility of a thinking of painting that avoids, on the one hand, the inevitable irony that occurs when self-reflexivity is taken to its logical extreme while, on the other hand, avoiding the apocalyptic celebration of painting's end. A similar point can be made in relation to the masking tape, the layering, the raised panels and the projected surfaces since, in every case, what is at work is the complex presence of painting and sculpture held within painting by the apart/a part. In sum, to the extent that this logic operates here in these examples, the object-in-question is affirmed because the question of the object is raised continually by the work's work. Once this questioning is positioned in relation to the traditional expectations of painting and sculpture — expectations that relate both to production and interpretation — the identification of the affirmed presence of the object-in-question will work to allow the reworking of painting beyond the determinations of tradition. Finally, therefore, in finding these other possibilities for Ryman's work to be already at work in his paintings, there is the possibility that the interpretive grid of modernism within which his worked is placed may have been loosened. With the slow release of that grip what comes to the fore is the work's work, once that work is understood as the continuity of enacting; a continuity formulated here in terms of the becoming-object.

*Jackson Pollock,* Number 1, 1950 (Lavender Mist), *1950, oil, enamel and aluminium on canvas, 221x299.7cm (reproduced courtesy of National Gallery of Art, Washington, Ailsa Mellon Bruce Fund)*

# Timed Surfaces: Jackson Pollock

Abstract expressionism as a movement, as a body of work, and as defining an area of historical and critical reception is already given. The figure of Pollock, a figure which at the very least allows both for paintings and a domain of critical engagement to be identified, is itself already present.[1] What is given as that within which these varying counters take place is a construal of modernism (and of modernity), the problem of interpretation — perhaps more exactly a questioning of the possibility of interpretation — and the site of a specific politics. The locus of any resistance to the given — a resistance that will be either real or putative — is itself therefore already in place. In eschewing a metaphysics of destruction, resistance — here another possibility for interpretation — will always have to work through the given. Prior to any attempt to take up what now emerges as a complex site there is a preliminary question that needs to be addressed. What marks out this questioning is that it seeks the justification of the strategy of resistance rather than the more straightforward formulation of the dynamics of resistance. The question of justification will hinge neither on a posited or assumed will to truth nor on the basis of an ethical imperative. A different claim is involved here; a claim of an-other order which will, in addition, in being taken up cause the basis of judgement to be rethought insofar as the nature of the object will have been repositioned. This other claim has two elements. In the first place it is that the given has necessarily failed to grasp the force of Pollock's work (a position argued for in many different quarters and which must always haunt interpretation). In the second place the way in which this force is to be uncovered will — in the uncovering of what is there — not only check the language of uncovering, truth as revelation, but show that what allows the reworking of the figure of Pollock, and thus that which sanctions the work's repositioning in terms of a fundamentally different ontological framework, is itself already at work providing the structuring force of Pollock's 'action paintings'. There is therefore a type of affirmation that is already effectively present in the formulation of this interdependence,

Affirmation is a stance in relation to the given in which critique (or an inherent critical possibility) and presentation come to be presented at one and the same time. (Their being copresent 'at the same time' is itself already the mark of a founding complexity. It is the complexity inherent in this position which can be identified as anoriginal complexity. The affirmation in question therefore will pertain here with this complex site. Moreover it will be complexity that is at work within and that works the surface of what are usually called the 'action paintings'.) There is a twofold implication inherent in this particular repositioning of these works. In the first place there is another take on the relationship between philosophy and art. In the second place it will work to indicate that the demands for continuity and thus the project of either metaphysical progress or historicism will have necessitated that the force working the frames be obviated. Natural time — namely history's time and therefore a time forbidding nature — demands that what is present with it be enclosed within it and in being ontologically simultaneous with what is present, be part of it. (Here the 'at the same time' necessarily precludes the possibility of anoriginal complexity.[2]) What this means is emphasising that the location of abstract expressionism demanded by the attempt to construct a continuous history of painting, must work to preclude the intrusion of the disruptive nature of these paintings. The disruption pertains to time and therefore is inextricably connected to the ontology of the art work. Disruption here is not the same as semantic undecidability. Reworking these paintings will have consequences for the writing of art's history. The preclusion of the paintings' force and the consequences of that reworking will combine to indicate not only what is at stake in any politics of aesthetics, but more significantly that what has to be taken up to reveal the political site is firstly the ontology of objects and secondly time. (The time in question will form an integral part of the process which is the becoming-object.) There will be an essential interarticulation here. Time, bringing its necessary ontological determinations with it, is significant precisely because disruption will involve a conflict between the temporality at work within the frame (the temporality working the action paintings) and the temporality of traditional historical time (sequential continuity) and with it of the temporality that this history demands of its objects in order that they form and inform part of that history.

Perhaps the difficult aspect of these claims — a difficulty that may inhere in the philosophical project itself — is the commitment to a claim about the nature of things; in this instance a claim about the modality of being proper to objects and the necessarily interarticulated presence of time. Furthermore the site of the claim, the history of painting coupled with the history of philosophical or theoretical writing about painting, will itself have to be presented as interarticulated with that thinking at the present which concerns itself — the concern exemplified by association or disassociation — with the ontology of timed objects. Implicated here are not objects of all sorts but, once again, objects of interpretation. It is this contextualising setting that needs to be taken up. Taking it up, and in so doing allowing it to be repositioned, will give rise not just to a reworking of the particularity of Pollock's work — and, even more, the particular within that work — but also to the more central claim to which allusion has already been made, namely that what will sanction both the possibility and the actuality of that reworking is itself already present — affirmatively present — within that which is at work in the work. As will be suggested the impossibility of the reduction, the pure state wanted by both Greenberg and Rosenberg, is due to the work of the object. It is the nature of the object — its coming to be present as an event — that defies simplicity. (Once more this is, of course, an ontological claim about the nature of objects.) Even though it is yet to be clarified in this context, integral to this undertaking will be the activity of work; in this instance the work of the work. With work and in the shift from an ontology of stasis to one involving process and movement, and thus with the subsequent situating of presentation within that interplay, it will then become possible to locate another time within what has been taken up to this point as a simply static site. The introduction of time turns the painting into that which will always include more than simply spatial determinations. The interplay of the horizontal and the vertical must yield time, perhaps yield to time. Again, the organising principle that guides this approach is the assumption that, as time and existence are necessarily interarticulated, ontological difference must be involved in any attempt to identify temporal difference.

The possibility of this reworking being already present does not involve an uncovering of a truth that had previously been covered or obscured. If anything is revealed it is the way in which the operation of tradition construes objects as having to be continuous with it. Revelation gives way to work since it is only via the activity of work that what is at work is able to be given again. There is no simple re-presentation; it is, rather, that what is at play is a repetition. Representation works with the static image which is regiven in a passage marked by both the essential passivity of the act and the necessary neutrality of the object within it. Neutrality here is the object always being the same as itself. Representation therefore is the necessary mode of the object's presentation given that the organising intention is writing a continuous history. Even if the history includes critiques and developments, representation endures if what is central is the representation of the 'same' object, the 'same' within the Same. Leaving to one side the possibility that representation is, in fact, a form of repetition — a repetition in and of the Same — what counters this construction is an-other possibility within repetition.[3] Maintaining the object as same and different is, in part, this other possibility. It will be in terms of this setup that the possibility of the interplay of giving and originality enacts, and is enacted by, the primordiality of repetition. (Parts of the work of the action paintings will be explicable in terms of the logic of the apart/a part.) One of the consequences that emerges from the recognition of the primordial presence of repetition is that the already present plurality within repetition itself is opened up, thereby denying any unity or self-referential identity to this 'itself'. There will be no repetition itself. There is no 'itself' as such. Singularity, therefore, will always need to be thought (and consequently rethought) beyond the purview of the suggested self-referentially singular. Singularity here will always be an after-effect of the event since the event becomes the name of anoriginal complexity. In this sense the event is the site of an initial irreducibility. Particularity or singularity involves either a form or decision that, whilst referring to the event, cannot enact the event as such.

It should not be too readily assumed, however, that this repositioning, reworking, repeating bears no relation to the given site. (Parenthetically, what will have to be taken up in a more systematic way is the temporality introduced and enacted by the prefix 're-'.) Indeed, what is of fundamental importance is how the relation is given and maintained. Here, as a point of departure, the provision of relation is held by the centrality of the interplay of object and interpretation. It is the object — or a formulation of the object — that dominates the initial reception. The primacy of the object — the pure and autonomous object — emerges with greatest clarity in the writings of Greenberg and Rosenberg. Connected to the question of the object there is the problem of interpretation; a problem nearly always advanced in terms of the possibility of interpretation. The importance of impossibility and negation, while paramount, will need to be given an-other context. In tracing the nature of the connection between the determination of the object and the question of interpretation, and the way in which they have a necessary interrelationship such that it is the posited purity and autonomy of the object that generates the interpretive problem, what will emerge from the process is that both the nature of the object and the act of interpretation will have an-other possibility. Part of the task at hand is giving some specificity to the alterity in question: how is this other possibility to be thought? Again, part of the answer will involve that which is already at work within the frame.

In writing *Towards a Newer Laocoon*, not only did Greenberg build on the distinctions identified earlier in *Avant-Garde and Kitsch*, but he also began to make a case for the unique nature of abstraction — and then for what in the end would be abstraction's purest expression — and in so doing he established the terrain for the investigation of future movements (and also moments) in the history of painting. As has been cogently argued, the haste with which the artistic and interpretive banner of post-modernism has been adopted begins as a rejection (whether it be recognised as such or not) of the basis of Greenbergian modernism.[4] In taking up the interpretive frames offered by Greenberg and to an extent by Rosenberg, what is essential is to locate that which gives their positions actual interpretive force. Both are concerned with a conception of purity, what is in fact a moving into self — and thus with autonomy, here the moving away from relation. Furthermore, in the case of Rosenberg, the significant element in his interpretation, for these present concerns, stems from the generalised description offered in *The American Action Painters* of the canvas, within abstraction, as an 'event'. While it will be necessary to return to this 'event' and with it to a more general consideration of the event, it is essential at this stage to note the way in which these varying positions are set up.

For Greenberg, what demarcates the avant-garde in the domain of the plastic arts from what he identifies as avant-garde poetry is that the former has been able to obtain 'a much more radical purity'. Greenberg constructs a number of important though nonetheless intriguing analogies in order to formulate the elements of this position:

> Painting and sculpture can become more completely nothing but what they do; like functional architecture and the machine they *look* what they *do*. The picture or statue exhausts itself in the visual sensations it produces. There is nothing to identify, connect or think about, but everything to feel.[5] [Original emphasis]

The analogy with functional architecture is significant in that, within the frame in which it is formulated and presented, not only does it raise Greenberg's enduring preoccupation with Kant, it also signals in what way the project of the avant-garde for Greenberg may harbour the pure object; perhaps in the end the purely minimal object. (Minimalism may have been the logical consequence of Greenberg's own arguments.) In harbouring the pure object what will come to be repeated is the dominant opposition of function and ornamentation. The instability of that distinction can be established by working through the analogy with functional architecture. The consequence of that work will be that emphasis will have to be given to looking — 'they *look* what they *do*' — and to experience; the latter incorporating both looking and feeling.

With the machine, however, something else is introduced. While the machine here is meant to suggest the purity of the process, it will be precisely this purity that will come to be belied by the machine's own work. It will be with the machine, and its already prefiguring work, that the centrality of process, repetition and the already present work of time will come to the fore. The consequence of these analogies will emerge by following the way in which Greenberg's conception of the avant-garde is developed and its object maintained. In so doing what must be retained as a question is the actual possibility of this reduction; work to machine. In retaining it as a question what is then also subject to a similar interpretive stance is everything that is implicated — assumed and presupposed — in the process of reduction. It will be with this questioning that the possibility of reduction — the envisaged pure state — will, in the end, have to be thought of as present (thus also as presented) with its impossibility.

Greenberg presents the avant-garde in painting in terms of what could be described as the continuity of surrendering and shedding; a generalised process of reduction. While there is an initial complexity in its formulation, it comes to be undone by the retention of the temporality of sequence and development; the temporality of historicism:

> The history of avant-garde painting is that of a progressive surrender to the resistance of its medium; which resistance consists chiefly in the flat picture plane's denial of efforts to 'hole through' it for realistic perspective space. In making this surrender, painting not only got rid of imitation — and with it, 'literature' — but also of realistic imitation's corollary confusion between painting and sculpture.[6]

There is therefore an attempt, identified by Greenberg, in the history of painting for the unfettered production of pure painting. What this involves can be provisionally presented in terms of a twofold move. In the first place it pertains to the internality of the frame; the application of paint to the canvas. It is here that the surface *qua* surface figures. In the second place there is the content of that surface. The content is the form of painting, the painting of figures, of that which, in Greenberg's sense of the term, imitates. Clearly these two domains are interrelated. Nonetheless for the moment it is important to trace the individual shedding and the specific reduction to and thus promulgation of a painterly 'radical purity'. The point of moving through the positions in this way is to allow the implicit conception of the object at work within them to emerge. It will be with the emergence of the positioned object that the possibility of repositioning, and thereby also of reworking the object, will arise. The element that will on the one hand allow the limit to be traced within Greenberg's conception of the surface while sanctioning, on the other, an intrusive and complex surface that will in the end check the argument that seeks to maintain autonomy as purity, is time. What will be argued is that with Pollock the surfaces are timed. Time is present working the frame. With the frame time is neither in it nor connected to it but, more emphatically, is constitutive of the work itself. In other words time forms a constitutive part of the work's work. Modernism's traditional construal as the place of the surface will be checked by this possibility.

In Greenberg's writings the argument concerning the surface is advanced with considerable precision. A continual description of the surface in terms of self-referentiality — 'brush strokes are often defined for their own sake' — is coupled with a view of the internality of canvas as creating life and as providing a world that is, or at least struggles to be, complete in itself. This latter point is clear from his formal description of the line:

> Line, which is one of the most abstract elements in painting since it is never found in nature as the definition of contour, returns to oil painting as the third colour between two other colour areas.[7]

The closed world of the frame is mirrored in the enclosing world of art. Its being enclosed is part of its autonomy. It should not be thought, however, that in the American context Greenberg was the only critic to argue for this sense of autonomy. Harold Rosenberg, as has already been suggested, when writing specifically about Pollock argues that what

> . . . was radically new about the method of the drips was that the method was all there was to them.[8]

Rosenberg went on to locate the primacy of what could be described as the enacted process of internality (Rosenberg's analogous term is 'inward action') in Newman, Smith and Still amongst others, in order then to state that what was at play in each was 'myth without myth content — a pure *state*' (original emphasis). Again there is the posited possibility of purity. The question that endures is the status of this singular state.

Autonomy and purity pertain to the work. Utilising the distinction between surface and content it becomes possible to argue that what is being suggested by the evocation of 'purity' is that not only will the frame house a world that is internally defined and regulated, but that such a world is itself only possible because of a complete separation of what is given within the frame from any other world. Peter Osborne has captured this precise point when he suggests that autonomy for Greenberg

> . . . is essentially a question of the degree to which a work has purified itself of any aesthetic content extrogenous to the formal properties of its particular physical medium.[9]

Internal regulation and definition means that the surface is constructed in terms of those conditions of possibility that are given by the surface. The use of one type of brush stroke as opposed to another, or one procedure for the application of paint as opposed to a different one, will always be determined by the relationships being constructed — perhaps to be constructed — within the frame. Once the work of the surface is defined in this way, the content of the work, necessarily, has to be coextensive with its being enacted. They become one and the same. The presence of an imitative impulse (again maintaining Greenberg's sense of imitation) has to be precluded as it would force into the frame a regulative principle from outside. What would be linked to the frame is an outside that positioned the frame as an inside such that the site of evaluation and judgement moved from the surface *qua* surface to a specific inside/outside relationship. Following the construal of autonomy under consideration here, what is immediately significant is the way in which this particular binary form is precluded from exercising a determining role in any interpretation of the frame. Greenberg can be read as alluding to the problem of the inside/outside when, in describing the possibility of indicating 'real objects' within the process leading to abstraction, he formulates it in the following terms:

> A vibrating tension is set up as the objects [real objects] struggle to maintain their volume against the tendency of the real picture plane to re-assert its material flatness and crush them to silhouettes.[10]

Here the work of the frame can be taken as enacting — or perhaps more accurately attempting to enact — the possibility of a form of autonomy. The relation to the outside is severed to the extent that the world of the frame is able to control and to regulate itself. If what is framed is a site of self-regulation in which relation is necessarily eschewed, then the question of the interpreted object will come to insist. What is it that is interpreted? What is it that is to be understood? What status is to be given to pure internality? In answering these questions it should be remembered that the absence of relation is the extruded mimetic possibility; the absent representational or imitative impulse.

The question of the object is inextricably linked to the activity of interpretation. In the case of Pollock this is inevitably the case. Rosenberg, in the passage already cited, establishes a coextensivity between the method of construction and the construction itself. A similar position is held by Greenberg. As soon as looking and doing are the same — recalls the passage '. . . they *look* what they *do*' — it is immediately clear that in describing the object what is given, and given at the same time, is an interpretation. Interpretation and description are necessarily linked. Once the link is established it then becomes possible to trace its consequences. On the one hand this can lead to the redescription of the paintings as no more than decoration, and on the other as destructive of the figure/ground relation that has been taken as dominant within Western art.[11] The task that arises is providing a more adequate approach to the object. The object will need to be repositioned in order that it can come to be reworked as an event.

As a point of departure it is essential to note that, as was intimated above, Rosenberg formulated the activity of the 'action painters' in general in terms of the event. As will be suggested, this formulation involves a particular construal of the event. It is one whose preconditions can be challenged.

> At a certain point the canvas began to appear to one American painter after another as an arena in which to act, rather than a space in which to reproduce, re-design, analyse or 'express' an object, actual or imagined. What was to go onto the canvas was not a picture but an *event*.[12] [My emphasis]

The contrast being drawn here by Rosenberg is rehearsed within this formulation in terms of the opposition between the painting as an event and the painting as an expression. The way towards an understanding of this particular use of the term expression is given by that which provides the temporal as well as the semantic synonymy of the terms 'reproduce', 're-design' and 'express'. The 're-' in this instance introduced a specific temporality. It is linked to the interdependency of surface and depth, and of simple and complex. Reproduction and redesigning (perhaps, in addition, redesignating) suggest an 'after' to which it is only possible to give priority on the basis of what is prior; the before rather than the after. The priority of the surface can only ever be justified in this instance — and thus can only come to be evaluated — because it is the re-presentation of something else; something which, while outside the canvas, outside because it is deeper, is given with the frame. The temporality here is marked by the process that generates the framed, the contents of the frame, as a subsequent moment in which an element that is temporally prior comes to be expressed or represented. It should not be thought that there is an actual presentation prior to re-presentation. It is rather that the frame is conceived as housing a surface that has depth rather than being a pure surface. Expression involves the expressed. Action, on the other hand, is thought to be pure and complete in itself. (The possibility of the pure is itself, in part, based on the posited immediate givenness of presentation; a possibility that, as will be argued, is even within its own terms impossible.)

The inscription, here, of the 're-' — the 're-' as the singular reiteration of expression — means that the surface brings with it a purported depth and consequently involves a division that must be given a temporal description. This has to be the case as the division in question involves what is neither coextensive nor simultaneous, from which it follows that the alterity in question is temporal as well as ontological. It is not just a spatial displacement. The representation cannot be designated as prior. On the contrary, it is the object that is reproduced or redesigned that is prior. The framed representation, therefore, even though it is recognised as such, is given as an after-effect which is parasitic, with regard to both semantics and value, on the priority of the prior. At work here are the varying permutations of representation. The distinction suggested by Rosenberg between expression and event needs to be situated within this particular frame, because, as a distinction, it can only function on the assumption that its components are reciprocally related. Representation brings with it the possibility that the depth demanded may come to be denied and therefore that the work of art, or object of interpretation, emerging as the result of this denial would be sheer presentation, pure givenness. Moreover, whatever force this eventuality may have it can only be derived from the denial of depth. (Posited depth bringing the outside into play turns the canvas into the site in which the opposition between inside and outside is taken as that which structures the site. What appears as a simple tautology is in fact the process of naturalisation.) And yet it must be asked: what is the denial of depth? Understanding both the event and Pollock's action paintings, their presence as events, will hinge upon recognising what is at work in this specific question. Indeed, it is possible and go further and suggest that advancing such a denial does itself turn upon maintaining the effective dominance of the opposition surface/depth. The abeyance of the effective presence of this opposition will, in this instance, result not in the vanishing but in the redemption of depth; depth will have been allowed an-other repetition. Depth will form part of the work — be a part of it — but only to the extent that it is apart from its traditional determinations. Even though they would have been placed beyond the purview of priority, both depth and surface would nonetheless be repeated; however, no longer as a functional opposition, their repetition would involve an-other difference (surface and depth retained within and for the logic of the apart/a part). In sum, the possibility that has been opened here is that the denial of the prior and of what either has or is given priority need not result in the immediate positing of the surface.

If the lead followed by what is implicit in Rosenberg's distinctions were taken, accepted as such, then the event would have to be construed as a pure surface; the site of self-regulation. The surface would emerge as the other possibility contained within the opposition surface/depth. The denial of depth could thus be interpreted as the assertion of the necessary unity and simplicity of the surface. The surface as an occurrence would be co-terminous with itself. (With this identification the event is denied.) The inside/outside opposition would, as has been suggested, no longer pertain. A way of formulating this state of affairs would be to argue that the surface has no depth and is therefore an undifferentiated process. Annette Cox's description of Pollock's work of this period utilises precisely this privileging of what turns out to be the unidimensional. It is of course a description that echoes, in part, the already offered purity and exclusive internality:

> With no hint of three-dimensional space, naturalistic elements, or even biomorphic shapes, Pollock reduced art to one of its essentials — the drawing of a line.[13]

However, this approach or mode of procedure will not work. The drawing in question is not the drawing of a line.

The line is not singular. It breaks the surface; marking and breaking it up at the same time. (Again, it will be necessary to return to this time of the 'at the same time'.) As two lines cross, they mark a marking out which is identified in the process without being reducible to the process. In other words a spacing comes to be placed within the frame by the simple presence of crossing lines inscribing, by marking, the presence of a difference. Spacing generates depth. The counter question must still be asked: could there be a way in which depth was denied? It may seem that, for example, Ryman's attempt to present the purity of colour — the undifferentiated field — closed the works off from an internal spacing. And yet this description will not suffice since both interpretive and material depth are present. The interpretive depth is the fundamental capacity for interpretive differential plurality that is contained by the object (by an object of interpretation) in terms of its having the quality of an event. The material depth does not involve space understood in terms of dimensions; but, rather, a spacing constructed as much by the temporal alterity introduced by the marks of painting, as by the process of framing in which the work of colour differentiates itself from the outside. Space becomes the mark of difference. In resisting self-unity — the unity of self with self that marks the reduction of presentation — difference allows depth another repetition by turning the surface into a site resisting assimilation. Here assimilation can be understood as self-absorption. It will be the impossibility of this absorption that on the one hand attests to the event while on the other demands to be thought of outside the realm of the melancholic and thus beyond any contemporary fascination with the *via negativa*.

It is in terms of this other repetition of depth that it becomes possible to interpret the dripping technique, and therefore the action paintings. Depth will become part of the surface. It is not disassociated from it as though it were the surface's counterpart. It works within the surface. Depth and surface working outside of the dominance of the logic of the either/or attest to the event; the event as being with depth. The repetition of depth beyond its traditional confines means that it is possible to discuss the action paintings in terms of an ontology of becoming without this necessitating the exclusion of presentation. Indeed it will obligate an-other thinking of presentation. If becoming were to be positioned with the opposition surface/depth then it would deny depth, with the result that the surface would become the site of its own being. The irony is that becoming would then have been denied. Once again it is the repetition of depth that introduces difference — irrecuperable difference — into the frame. It is introduced by being marked as such. The mark differs and hence difference, as marking its own introduction, can never be the same as itself.

Presentation taken as the interrelated presence of surface and depth attests in the first place to the plurality of the event. The event becomes the site over which interpretive dominance can never be asserted in any absolute sense. Secondly it is the apart/a part presence of surface and depth that serves not as the prelude to interpretation but as part of the interpretive act itself. In paintings such as *Lucifier*, *No 1*, *Full Fathom Five*, *Lavender Mist*, what becomes important is not the dripping as the mark of a process nor the conjectured supremacy of chance over design (a position in which chance would be no more than design's other and thus not chance at all), but the more ordinary, and yet potentially more significant, overlaying of paint. It is this which constitutes a site whose potential, and indeed whose depth, appears to be infinite. The surfaces while present break down. They generate neither an unending surface nor an undifferentiated complexity. Surfaces play out onto other surfaces. The relationship between them is established, as was suggested, by that overlaying of paint which has the consequence of opening different and unpredictable spaces within the frame. It is a process of overlaying that will resist archaeological analysis. Rather than being a simple multiplicity in unity (though nor is it, for that matter, unity arising out of multiplicity), what the frame contains is the affirmed presence of the event; an event with depth. The recovery of the event is an act that only becomes possible within the temporality of interpretation. What is constructed within the process of interpretation is the already present irreducibility that is sustained and enacted within the matter of the painting. Here it is the work's material presence that is fundamental to the work's work.

The event can no longer be said to take place in contradistinction to expression. It therefore does not have the temporality that allows representation, as classically construed, to take place. The temporality of the event is originally — thus anoriginally — complex. Within any painting the copresence of a number of different possibilities means that the actual relationship between narrative and time that is to be found in writing cannot pertain. (How this absence is to be understood is, however, the question.) The process of dripping is physical. It involves the placing of lines over lines. The lines themselves are swirls, drops, blocks running into blocks. Starting at any point the path begun runs across as well as down. Sections and intersections are created and denied; threads end to start again; what was obscured becomes that which itself obscures. These movements depend upon the interplay of surface and depth; of one with and within the other. What, therefore, is there to be seen? While the cartographical impulse may be strong — strong in terms of its suggesting a possible field of interpretation, the mapped unconscious — a painting such as *Lavender Mist* neither maps a site, a place, though nor does it present the non-place. In order to locate what occurs in the place of these two no longer pertinent possibilities, it will be necessary to stay with the negative. What is at work here is neither a synthesis nor a sublation. The question that insists will therefore concern placing that which is neither the giving of place nor its denial. The opening and closing that is the intersection, the crossing, the abutment, the obscuring, the curtailing, the extending, etc, created by colour and line (one and both, coloured lines, lined colour) works to create a site that resists synthesis: the negative still pertains. The resistance and the negative need to be given a more precise determination. Part of that precision will involve what was alluded to above in terms of 'apart/a part'; and which is therefore to be traced through the working of the logic of the apart/a part.

Synthesis is narrative. It is the attribution to the canvas of a story. Narrative, as a beginning, is sequential time. The resistance and with it the projected impossibility of synthesis — itself already an integral part of the work's work — do not mean that what is present is atemporal. It is rather that the temporality of narrative is no longer apposite; another time will insist. With a narrative the temporal structure demands that a location be given. In painting the equivalent to the beginning in a written narrative is provided either specifically by the painting's focal point or more generally by perspective. Access is given, and given with it are the expectations concerning the content of the given. How is it possible to begin *Lavender Mist*? There would be little point arguing that the question of the beginning does not pertain; the painting, after all, will have been seen. Furthermore, any description of the internality of the frame must locate a point of departure. The absence of narrative, given that this does not make the frame — the content of the frame, the frame at work — atemporal, will yield this other time. What is enacted in the interplay of lined colour and coloured lines, in the presence of configurations — not figures — that mark out a process beyond synthesis? What, then, is held apart? Of what does that which is held apart form a part?

Answering these questions must begin with the recognition that the world evoked by the title — *Lavender Mist* — is of a semantic and ontological setup that is systematically denied by the work of what has been framed. There is nothing beneath the mist. No clear view that has become obscured. The title betrays the work by naming the presence of the traditional interplay of surface and depth. Moreover it raises the spurious possibility of the painting's truth being given via a revelation occurring in and as a clearing. Here, on the contrary, there is nothing obscure; in fact there is no mist. What is present — and what it is that is presented — continues to be given; affirming thereby the primordiality of process and, with it, of work. Precisely because of this shift in what is taken as primordial — a move from stasis to becoming — it is possible to argue that, rather than there being the given object, there is a related change in which what emerges is the becoming-object. Within that object the impossibility of a focal point and therefore of a synthesising vision means that the divisions, the spacings, within the frame that work to create a discontinuity of continuous connections, reinforce the instability of vision. By allowing for an-other possibility for surface and depth, the logic of the a part/apart works to create an internal spacing; a spacing that, in giving the already plural, positions the framed as a plural event.

There are, therefore, at least two senses in which it is possible to suggest that the surface is timed. The first is the temporality at work within the frame; the temporality of giving. Giving is simply, to begin with, what is given to be seen. This gift to sight cannot be automatically construed in terms of the optical for that would be to allow the frame to be presented in spatial terms. Rather than the enclosed temporality of narrative, the fact that it is possible, as it were, to begin at any point and what will be traced from that point will connect only to disconnect with other tracings from other points, means that a temporality sustaining the complete with the incomplete — one working to maintain the other — will be needed in order to take up the work of the work. The second is the time of complex repetition. Despite the obvious plurality when these two times are brought together (it is of course already possible to take their copresence as descriptive of the work's complex work) their internal work also precludes the possibility of a final and thus also original all-encompassing synthesis; there is an anoriginal irreducibility. This is the strength of the counter desire for historical unity. Within the historicist purview, the internality of the work, its content, must be complete and completely given at a time that can readily be identified. Time and completion are necessarily connected. The enforcing of a temporal simultaneity — a simultaneity imposed after the event which denies the event — would have allowed the content to form a part of history; the sequential time of continuity and thus a movement in which both time and object would have been involved in a reciprocity of simultaneity. One would be simultaneous with the other and the simultaneity of one (ontologically) sustains its being simultaneous with the other (temporally). Ontological and temporal completion mark out the status of the object. What is sundered by the work of the work is precisely this setup; indeed, allowing for the frame's other work is the way in which spacing becomes timed and time allows for its own being spaced. Occurring at the same time reinforces the presence of anoriginal complexity; painting's other possibility. What can no longer be sustained, therefore, is depth as that which provides art with its truth. Depth was from the start a ruse posed for art by a philosophical thinking dominated by the ontology and temporality of representation; tradition's inevitable work. The truth of art is neither on the surface nor is it in its depth. Positing the centrality of the surface, even a play of surfaces, is the banal and nihilistic gesture of the counter move to depth; positing met by counter positing. The truth of art will involve the capacity to mark the presence of surface and depth; again a complex copresence. This is the recognition of a difference that precludes by obviating the possibility of a synthetic totality. As a beginning the action paintings can be located at this site. As works of art they are demanding. With this demand it is possible to return to the image of the machine and the possibility of purity. The connection with Ryman will also emerge at this precise point.

Rosenberg's evocation of the event and Greenberg's equation of action painting with functional architecture are linked to the possibility of original purity and thus with a founding simplicity. Functional architecture, it is said, resists ornamentation and therefore is simply itself; pure utility. Similarly, it is said that the machine does what it is intended to do; it is therefore pure function. The coextensivity between form and function that works the machine and that is at work within functional architecture, it is conjectured, is the analogue of what is taking place within these paintings. There are two reasons, however, why this is not the case. The first is that it misconstrues the paintings. The second is that, equally, it misconstrues both functional architecture and the machine. Once it becomes possible to argue that ornamentation is to be understood as part of the building's logic and is thus neither an addition nor a supplement; furthermore, once it can be claimed that function does not exist *tout court*, but is necessarily relative such that it is possible to take up the question of function's own function; finally, once it becomes possible to rethink the machine such that form and function may be held apart (be this thinking futural or actual), then all of these possibilities introduce an inevitable complexity. Function will involve an inescapable doubling causing the opposition between function and ornament to be recast. The recasting and the doubling mark out the specific work of anoriginal complexity. To the extent, therefore, that complexity is sanctioned the event endures and with its endurance it then becomes possible to re-establish the analogy, this time in terms of the ontology and temporality of the event. While the analogy will endure at one level it is sundered at another. What cannot be maintained is the specificity of the art object as having an analogy with either the machine or functional architecture. The particularity of art work holds itself apart; its demands are different.

*Anselm Kiefer*, Nero Malt (Nero Paints), *1974, oil on canvas, 220x300cm (reproduced courtesy of the artist)*

# Placing History: Anselm Kiefer

It is not as though the paintings of Anselm Kiefer turn around the interplay of history, memory and representation. It is, rather, that these three topics provide what comes to be framed within the paintings as their own proper topos; and, within that topos, their presence is complicated.[1] At work within the field of painting they provide the paintings with their work. What this will mean is that the paintings draw on and utilise the resources that inhere in memory, history and representation. The specificity of their work, however, is connected to what occurs when these resources are themselves put to work. In this move their assumed determinations — the already given particularity of memory, history, and representation — no longer dominate and even though these resources need to be understood as bringing with them, and hence enacting, the material presence of tradition, what is enacted takes the form of a questioning rather than a painterly or interpretive *fait accompli*. In sum their movement into work is traversed by a questioning of memory, history and representation. This questioning which comes to be at work in the frame thereby forms an integral part of the work's work. And yet this questioning does not stem from idle speculation, it is rather a questioning that, once recognised, forms an insistent part of the present. Kiefer reworks and redeploys the problems already inherent in the history of representation in order to allow for a refiguring of representation after the Shoah.[2] The Shoah within Kiefer's work — the work of a German painter part of whose project turns around the question of what possibility art has after the Shoah — is not a topic to be addressed as though it were outside occupying a neutral space. On the contrary, by allowing the Shoah the space occasioned by its present remembrance, this will mean that it has to work to structure the space of memory, history and representation. It will be remembrance — a remembrance itself already constitutive, in part, of the present — that must defer and defray the work of forgetting.

Forgetting involves a particular stance in relation to history. The content of that history, even if it is yet to be specified, works as has been suggested within the present. It is the nature of that work, and the conception of the present articulated therein, that opens a way towards an understanding not only of the stakes of active forgetting, but of its possible overcoming. The work of history, as with work in general, demands a presentation in which the actative rather than the substantive dimension should be emphasised. Within the work of Anselm Kiefer the overcoming of an intended forgetting is connected to a more general problem. Initially it concerns representation: the conception of what it is that comes to be represented and thus is given to be the representation. Historical detail does not form the subject matter to be represented. The represented — a term whose designation is still to be clarified — has a twofold presence, one which demands its own constitutive doubling or repetition. The occurrence will always involve an initial determination constructed by the relationship between representation within the frame and the frame as representation. (Both are, of course, always potentially delimited by an internal series of frames.) The frames do not simply mediate presence, they sustain it, and in so doing comprise part of the event's work, its productive presence as the event.

Identified here are a number of preliminary problems and areas of investigation. However, they are only preliminary in terms of their generality. They do not precede Kiefer's work and as such do not form an approach to it. They approach it only insofar as they are already operating within the work. The pre-liminary is not to be located 'before', as though it led to the frame. The paintings do not exemplify generality. There is a sense in which general concerns are enacted by them, with the consequence that the generality (and therefore any recourse to it or identification of it) will exist as an after-effect. Generality will have become a trope of the work: the work of Kiefer's approaches. The temporality of the 'preliminary', of that which is prior to — on but before the edge — will need to be rethought in relation to an envisaged doubling. This doubling is a repositioning of the general in terms of the particularity of content. The paintings, as paintings, can no longer be thought of in terms of their being exemplary. The paintings do not exemplify. They are only examples of that which comes to be presented as their content. And yet that content is never simple. Part of the placing of this opening, its being placed within the movement of interpretation, will involve the logic of the a part/apart. It will incorporate by providing the space of doubling. Doubling will be a necessary copresence that marks out an original, and therefore anoriginal site of complexity.

Despite the difficulty inherent in the act of interpretation, a difficulty that will always necessitate caution, there is little difficulty concerning the approach to be taken to these frames. The arbitrary comes to be restricted in two specific ways. The first concerns the overdetermined historicity of any approach, its figuring within and thus in some sense already figuring tradition. (They *are* paintings.) The second is the inscription of the ineliminable historical presence — and therefore of a necessary historicity — within the frame. (There *is* an already present — thus presented — content.) This inscription takes place in the form of sites: mythological figures, named landscapes, historical characters, actual occurrences, etc. However, the inscription of history is not reducible to these sites even though it is present within them. The sites form part of works that are always delimited by the active work of framing both within the painting and of the painting. While it will need to be indicated in greater detail both instances are mediated by their presence within the logic of the apart/a part. Framing presented in this way has two different types of relationship with representation. On the one hand, there is the setting for representation, and on the other there is the setting of representation. In other words, what comes to be framed is the interplay (though the exact nature of this interplay remains to be determined) between the sites as representations and the standing of representation itself. What this will mean is that representation, far from being taken as an end in itself — an end governing and determining the place and space of presentation — will be, within the frame, subject to analysis and examination. Representation will become an object of investigation within the frame such that the investigation, that is its own presentation, will have to figure as a fundamental and to that extent inescapable part of the work's work. The complex presence of representation is enacted in a number of different ways. Here two different though interrelated moments of painting will be taken up. The first brings the question of painting to the fore, the second turns around the question of painting's difficult relationship to representation and thus in this instance to history. With both what comes to be questioned is the problematic of representation and memory; a questioning which, as with Boltanski, could only have taken place after the Shoah. While the consequence of this questioning will be taken up, what needs to be noticed in passing is that the consequence of the continuity of questioning — painting taking up the question of its own possibility by figuring the questioning of representation and memory — works to maintain the work of these paintings. What this means is that the object understood as the object-in-question plays a determining and therefore affirmed role in these works. The assumed finality, both temporal and interpretive, of the object gives way to a process in which activity is always being completed. Work continues.

### Painting, Placing

The site of representation, a site that brings with it its consequent entailments thereby repositioning and reworking the site in terms of complexity, is enacted as a (re)presentation that displaces the centrality of representation. In the case of *Nero Paints*, *Painting=Burning* and *Icarus — March Sands*, an important part of this enactment is the palette, the floating and/or winged palette. These paintings, the first two completed in 1974 and the latter in 1981, have been the subject of different and conflicting interpretations. At this stage the emphasis will be given to the first two paintings. One general interpretation — general since it would have to include both these early works and, for example, the more recent (1987) *Milky Way* — is that the scorched earth and the distant building allude to or evoke a world that art will come to transcend, and, in transcending it, will redeem the fallen world. Art would emerge, therefore, as the transcendental source and site of redemption. In the case of *Nero Paints*, it is argued that both emperor and artist have similar aspirations of dominance, to which it would be added that they both destroy, with the consequence that a new order may arise to take the place of the old. While the problem of the secondary representation and thus the possible painterly *mise en abîme* is never addressed in interpretations of this kind, what is also overlooked is the content as well as the contact of the palette.

The presence of the palette within works of art already has a long and detailed history. The palette, as presenting painting, necessitates its own inscribed presence as holding paint; it presents another hold on painting. The palette would therefore generally be painted to contain the paint which would come to be used in painting. The potential for painting is painted onto the canvas. It is made present. With Kiefer, however, in these works, not only is the palette empty, it also works to frame and, in framing, to gesture towards the limits — perhaps the preliminary — and thus to provide a type of border. Therefore there is more involved here than the simple presentation of painting's possibility. The palette is not just the inscription of art — the means of its own production — into and as the work of art. Its presence is in addition, though this is by no means a simple addition, to the presence of the problem of frames, limits and borders. The addition becomes the framing of representation and in framing it, in its being presented, representation becomes, within the work of presentation, subject to an analysis of its own possibility and determinations. In a quite specific sense, therefore, representation is a part of yet apart from itself by its having been taken up into the work as a part of the work's work. This complex scene reworks and therefore repositions the palette such that the absence of held paint becomes the mark of a different present; a difference that repositions identity by checking any obvious identification of the painting's source and thus the source of painting. There is no origin of the work of art.

What is important is the nature of the absence, the sense of emptiness; yet it goes without saying that the empty palette is, in addition, not empty. Part of what it frames is the burnt field. The framing, however, is not an enclosing. The palette opens up a field of inquiry. In the case of *Nero Paints*, part of what the palette touches are houses either lit by the paintbrush as taper, or painted, as blazing, by the paintbrush as paintbrush. The brushes become the site of a productive irreducibility which will figure as a descriptive paradox.[3] The presence of paradox as presenting the irreducible is compounded by the presence of the palette. For the fire that is linked to the brushes/tapers is fuelled by the palette placed over the burnt field. The field as the site is marked and framed (the incomplete nature of this framing will be significant) by the palette. The palette, therefore, while part of the painting, is apart from the presented site in that it is also present as the site of representation, its setting. The palette constructs an opening within the frame: a spacing. The paintbrush/taper yielding a descriptive paradox, itself the mark of an ineliminable irreducibility, and the palette as a part yet apart, work to plot the limit of description, and thereby of any posited formalism. What is can no longer be described in terms of a synthetic unity; a repetition governed by the Same. Description of the site/sites only attests to paradox and to spacing by bringing with it, and thus enacting, a plurality that is not simple diversity. Description reaches its limit in the positioning of a spacing that gives rise to judgement; and, here, what is meant by judgement is the response to anoriginal plurality. It is the necessity for a decision or for an enacted possibility that recognises the role of the infinite within finitude. It positions itself as a completion that will never complete. Spacing and the appearance of paradox are also at work in the burnt field. The field as the site of renewal will not just be used again, but again and anew. The site therefore becomes one of repetition or, to be more precise, a site for that conception of repetition which only sustains the same by differentiating it from itself. Repetition, in this sense, once again breaks from the rule of the Same, for it now involves the unruly copresence of an identity (the again) and difference (the anew).[4] Merely seeing the field as the site of renewal limits the work of repetition, in that the landscape is reduced to the simple presence of landscape and therefore, as was suggested, to a repetition of the Same. Repetition governed by the Same posits an intentional trajectory of description. The repetition of genre is constrained to exclude any element that would work against the effectivity of generic repetition, which here would mean that if the generic repetition is articulated within the Same, what is then precluded is the possibility of another repetition in which even though the genre is maintained (it is given again) it does not preclude, indeed it will sanction, its being present in an as yet to be determined way. The copresence of the two — the presence of that which is given as irreducible — will mean that what will insist within the presentation of landscape is the ineliminable presence of the presentation as question; in other words the presentation is present in terms of the object-in-question.

While their detail remains to be clarified, it is the interarticulation or copresence of the 'again and anew' on the one hand, and the 'apart yet a part' on the other, that provides a frame for an interpretation of *Nero Paints* and *Painting=Burning*. (It should be added of course that their interpretation will have already commenced.) Again, the preliminary is never before the limit, where that limit is the frame of interpretation. This interpretive frame does not contain a grid within which the paintings can come to be placed and thereby mapped. The interarticulation alluded to above is already present, and not just in the frame. It is both subject to the frame and the frame's subject. To which it could be added that paradox as an opening — a spacing — gives rise to the possibility of accounting for the difference between the two above-mentioned forms of repetition. The difference here is, though perhaps with a certain irony, the paradoxical one between Nero and painting. (The possible irony is that both appear within and thus as a painting.) If it can be assumed that the houses burning in *Nero Paints* can be viewed as the result of Nero's actions, then this fire needs to be distinguished from the fire marking the burnt fields. The first form of fire — Nero's — is the nihilism of a projected pure destruction. It is not nihilistic because of the destruction but because of the projection. Here the projection involves both pure destruction and absolute renewal. What is necessarily precluded from such a setup, therefore, is relation. Nihilism becomes the denial of relation's primordiality. It is a denial that is countered by affirmation in which the determinations of a metaphysics of destruction are no longer operative; another mode of thinking will have taken place. Part of the affirmation of relation is that it signals the acceptance of the inevitability of history — the ineliminable presence of the work of tradition — while at the same time resisting the reduction of the present to a moment of historical continuity.

The consequence of the disassociation of fires means that, while painting may equal burning, the painter is not Nero. The title *Nero Paints* identifies, names, a division within the painting. The title as naming division, taken in relation to the palette, the burning houses and the scorched fields, works to differentiate two types of artistic activity, two different intentional logics,[5] and finally two types of fire. Fire is linked to representation. As such it raises both political and ethical questions for, as is known, the fire of destruction cannot touch remembrance. It can destroy, and that which has been destroyed cannot be represented as such. But remembrance is announced from the position of the witness who is vigilant in relation to what defies or precludes its own representation. Vigilance in this sense envisages a responsibility. It opens onto and enjoins present remembrance. The point that must be recognised is that the two types of fire, and all that they bring with them, do not simply inform the painting. On the contrary, they are part of what forms it. While the presence of the two fires will be pursued, what needs to be examined, as an opening move, is their relation to a deliberate forgetting.

In outline, this form of forgetting involves a conception of history in which relation comes to be suppressed. Relation, however, is not continuity; at least not a simple continuity. By relation what is envisaged is a type of repetition. The fire of destruction aims at elimination, absence without memory: a destructive disavowal in which any renewal is premised upon a complete overcoming of the disavowed object. What is given is given such that its existence can be subjected to that form of negation the operation of which intends to abnegate its repetition. That which is will be no more. Willed repression becomes the form taken by metaphysical destruction. The fire of destruction depends upon — because it also articulates — a certain ontology of objects. (Here objects is to be given its largest possible extension: objects in this sense incorporates both sites, historical locations, occurrences and finally the event.) The reference to ontology will allow for the distinction between the fires to be reworked in terms of difference such that the canvas becomes the site of an interplay of a differential ontology. The fire of destruction identified in *Nero Paints* posits an object situated within the ontology of a delimited stasis. It is structured by and articulated within that mode of being in which the object comes into existence and after which it can cease to exist. Both of these moments exist in chronological time. In other words, existence here involves a temporality of sequential continuity. These moments can be fixed and to that extent dated. The last date — the final point in the sequence — marks the moment at which destruction occurs. Even though dating and fixing are open to a questioning that strikes at their very possibility, it is nonetheless still the case that the intended obliteration of the event is the intention to end presence. However, this end is only possible if obliteration is at the same time marked by active forgetting. Here, forgetting is not simply the denial of both repetition and remembrance; it also involves the refusal of responsibility, where responsibility is understood as involving vigilance. (This is why questions of amnesty need to be differentiated from any form of amnesia.) The question posed by active forgetting — the question of how its potential can be maintained while its actuality is overcome — is addressed by the other fire, since within it obliteration is also announced. Here, however, something else is taking place since, henceforth, destruction — the intended obliteration — involves a different logic. Before taking it up, it is essential to note that their difference, and hence their relation, a relation of difference, and the related spacing it involves, form and inform the frame, and thus in part work to comprise the site of judgement. (The latter is sited because of the ineliminable and yet effective presence of irreducibility.) What is at stake here is that, as difference emerges, all that description can ever accomplish is a re-presentation of that emergence. It is precisely this irresolvability on the level of description (namely, the impossibility of a description that encompasses the totality of that which is framed) that points towards judgement. While the nature and the content of that judgement is a separate problem, the necessity for its occurrence marks the limits of description. (Description's limit will have its analogue in the limit of pure materiality.)[0]

Returning to the field of repetition, the first element that must be noted is the presence of landscape. This repetition is true for a large number of Kiefer's paintings. The landscape yields a field of interpretation and yet the field is not a landscape. The generic repetition gives the field. It is given as the site of destruction. It is, however, a site that only endures when, and if, this endurance is linked to painting. Painting figures as the setting of representation, presented by the palette in its being part of the painting. The repetition of landscape presents a site that is neither a simple landscape nor just the locus of history. Identifying it as such would present it as no more than a historical landscape. This form of presentation would seek to actualise that distancing that begins to broach forgetting. The presentation of the field as the site of history, history's actual geography — a site articulated within the logic of the again and anew, here beginning with the repetition of landscape — in this instance gives rise to a reversal of this movement. This reversal arises out of the projected overcoming of the reduction to landscape. The abeyance of genre breaks the hold of the merely historical, and by freeing landscape introduces history as the work of remembrance. In addition, while distancing is maintained, its maintenance is construed or presented in terms of the necessary obligation of a relation to the distanced. Remembrance is enacted within the painting in terms of the logic of the again and the anew. Present remembrance is to be differentiated from simple memory in which the object loses effectivity and, in so doing, could never involve the distanced relation that is not a simple mourning but a present insistence. Remembrance within repetition retains that relation but construes remembrance as present, where that presence and the presence of the occurrence of remembrance will always involve a difference that precludes the twin poles of a full or empty present. Remembrance's occurrence will incorporate its hold on that which is given to be remembered. It is the already present incompleteness that gives rise to vigilance and thus to responsibility; and it should be added that there is a fundamental link between this presentation of responsibility and hope. Hope does not end action. On the contrary, it becomes the end of action; an end that is present. It may, in addition, indicate that hope will demand a more complex structure and a different temporality in which, rather than being given a necessarily futural dimension, hope becomes a constitutive part of the present.

Returning to the fires what has emerged is that differentiating itself from the logic of

*Anselm Kiefer*, Ikarus — Märkischer Sand (Icarus — March Sands), *1981, oil, acrylic, emulsion, shellac, sand on photo on canvas, 290x360cm (reproduced courtesy of the artist)*

obliteration and the ontology of a delimited stasis is the logic of the again and anew. The difference in question is not the simple opposition between being and becoming. It is rather that the again and the anew involve a different construal of becoming: one in which there must be the continual non-excluding presence of the given — the field, the genre of landscape — and its being given again. The again entails the anew. Their copresence means that it is ontological difference that sustains the logic of the again and anew, since the difference of which it is comprised is irreducible on the level of ontology. The complex that this engenders is a site — a frame — that resists synthesis on at least two levels. The first is the difference between the fires. One is presented — at least on the level of intentional logic — in terms of an ontology of stasis; while the other demands an ontology of becoming. Their copresence is of course the nature of the work's work. Here what this provides is a specific and therefore regional indication of the way in which the work works both in terms of the becoming-object as well as the object-in-question.

The title *Painting=Burning*, coupled with the painting itself, brings to the fore the work of remembrance. The title posits an identity. The work of the 'equals' sign would seem to establish an equivalence. However, the identity is complicated by its formality; 'Painting' and 'Burning' remain without content. The use of the term formal and the recognition of an initial absence of content should not be seen as alluding to a division between the transcendental and the practical, as though content could be given to the equation in the move to experience. Were this to be the case, then the practical would in some way hold the truth of the formal proposition. The title names the difference already identified as the copresence of the two fires in *Nero Paints*.[7] In the example of that particular painting it was their copresence that introduced a difference that demanded judgement by enacting its conditions of possibility. Present remembrance involved the overcoming of Nero's painting. Here painting does not exist as an end in itself. Transcendent art cannot be privileged or seen to be privileged in Kiefer's work. His approach is different. In the case of *Painting=Burning*, an approach would need to be made in terms, firstly, of the title (and the problems of the equivalence invoked by it); secondly, of the palette as a part yet apart; and thirdly, of the burnt field as the field of repetition. One conclusion to be drawn here is that the concepts and categories that structure interpretation in terms of either genre or pre-given sites are no longer adequate. The question of what is adequate needs to be re-posed such that any response to it, and subsequent interpretation of it, will not work to eliminate the spacing at work within the frame.

In *Icarus — March Sands*, a space is opened by an intriguing reversal. In this painting the palette, while empty, is given a type of content by having a wing. The legend of Icarus would seem to figure in a direct way. It is announced in the title and present in the wing. However, the specificity of the legend introduces a complicating factor. In it Icarus refused to take any notice of the advice offered by his father Daedalus. His flight thus brought him close to the sun. The wax on his wings began to melt and he fell to earth. The problem here is the location of the fire. In the painting it is the March Sands that are on fire. Has Icarus already fallen, falling back to a fiery place? Or does the fire work to remove the possibility of the legend's flight and hence give rise to a fall before the fall? What is at stake in trying to resolve the problem of fire and its relation to Icarus? In the first place, if the burning sands had robbed him of his flight, such that even if he is only aloft for a moment, then this takes place beyond or at least distanced from a spatial equivalent to transcendence (understood as the turn to utopia), and what emerges as central is the relationship between art and the burning sand as a topos. The topos, in undoing transcendence, has become the place of politics and therefore of another history. (Here history is no longer to be identified with history's geography.) However, this could only occur if the March Sands are no longer those March Sands present within and thus reducible to an instance within the genre of landscape, but are repeated such that they become both the March Sands of landscape and the site of history; what is at work here is once again what has been designated as the again and the anew. Here the Sands are present as both. Furthermore, 'Icarus' in the title must name both Icarus and the setting of representation. Even the proper is not limited by its propriety. It must name 'that' and more. Its limitation lies in the always-to-be-determined relation that takes place between the two. Presented in this way, there is no need to choose between the questions since the second concerns the impossibility of rising above the site of history; the event of the place. Mythology is not to be opposed to the historical. While the precise nature of their relation is not given within the frame — it is, of course, an open question whether or not the frame could even contain such an abstraction — what is nonetheless countered is the presentation of mythology as in some sense either prefiguring history or as overcome by history's subsequent truth. The question in that precise sense therefore comes to be answered by the consequences of the interplay of what has been identified thus far in terms of the again and the anew and the logic of the apart/a part. Both are grounded in and thus become the work of a differential ontology.

## Margarete, Shulamite

There are a group of paintings that return to the figures of Margarete and Shulamite. What is of interest is that around which this return turns. In one of these works there is a line of painting; painted words. And yet what is painted, in being painted and in becoming words, differentiates itself from painting. The technique of the same breaks with itself in becoming painting, breaking while remaining painting; apart yet a part. It is thus that painting can work as the questioning of representation — and the entailments of representation — while holding to presentation and thus while presenting. Again what returns is the object-in-question. Furthermore there is the related demand that relation comes to be rethought, with the result that such a rethinking may cause relation to be taken as central. In Kiefer's painting *Your Golden Hair, Margarete,* the line written into the frame also works to frame. Despite the necessity of the 'also', this work — the line's work — is neither a simple addition nor a supplement. Work here attests to the anoriginal plurality of the line when construed as an event. (It is here, of course, that Pollock's line intersects with Kiefer's.) The words cut the furrows — cutting them by cutting across them — thereby providing another horizon. (This 'another' while denoting an addition is a further presentation within an already existing plurality.) The painted words work therefore in different ways. Their working works beyond the confines established by the supplementary. The other horizon neither adds nor compliments. It opens by reopening the site of interpretation.

The difference is both announced and maintained by the combination of painting and words. It is this combination that effaces the possibility of a reduction, within any putative interpretation, of paintings to words. The line in this painting, 'Dein goldenes Haar, Margarethe' (Your golden hair, Margarete), is in addition (again an addition which resists the import of a simple addition) to its being a line, an as yet to be specified citation, the painting's title. The problem of names and titles thereby ensues. Here, this problem will remain by being introduced — perhaps reintroduced — within citation; the other site of naming. The presence of the line is, on one level at least, unproblematic. It is taken from Paul Celan's poem *Todesfugue*. (It will be seen, however, that the singularity of this 'it', the line, is already, from the start, open to question.) The citation, within the already given frame, raises quite specific questions. They pertain to the site of citation. The site is, of course, the framed area. However, as has already been indicated, the words also frame. The words, the line, occur five times in the actual poem. What, therefore, has been cited? Which line? Which one — which instance — comes to be sited in the painting? The difficulty of answering these questions is not derived from any epistemological shortcomings or hindrance. (Here it is a difficulty approaching impossibility though redefining impossibility in the movement towards it.) Indeed the contrary is the case since the setting of a limit to any particular frame of questioning is in itself significant; a significance that is neither delimited nor enclosed by the established limit. The emergence of limits works therefore to open citation, thereby indicating that there is more at stake here than a simple repetition. Furthermore, a consequence of this opening is that there can no longer be either a direct or unproblematic answer to the question: which line has been cited? While the question of specificity may appear, as a question, to be apposite, its pertinence is lacking because its force depends upon its having been formulated within the frame established by the logic of identity. The question intends to pick out a single answer. Its scope is limited from the start. It goes without saying that the specific instance of this line will open up to include all lines. Identity and its prevailing logic will cede its place to another thinking that repositions identity beyond the sway of this logic. Here the citation takes place with repetition, thereby allowing for a more generalised move involving a reconciliation of all citations falling within the province of repetition.[8]

If it were thought that all that was at play within the general frame were words and their repetition — the intended singularity — then the repetition in question would involve the repetition of the same. (Care must be taken here for while the 'Same' may include identity, it can never be reduced to it.) This particular construal of repetition has its sources in what could be described as a formalised Platonism. It endures as that element of the Platonic tradition within which that conception of mimesis proper to the strategy of Plato's dialogues (proper in the sense of intended) remains as a determining and structuring influence. What such a conception of mimesis will always involve — involvement as consequence — are the problems that come to the fore within the attempted 'giving again' of that which had already been given. The mimetic structure does not necessitate the presence of a Platonic 'idea', for what is at work here is an already abstracted logic of mimesis. As abstracted it reworked, and with that work repositioned, as the more general problematic of representation. The abstractions remove the centrality of the ideal and its ontological and temporal role, but nonetheless retain the formal problem posed by the presenting, hence re-presenting, of that which has already been presented. The problem stems, as the formulation indicates, from the posited centrality of the image. The image is articulated within the terms set by the ontology of stasis; here involving the assumed singularity of identity. In other words the image, when taken at a remove, opens up the problem of its own authenticity. This authenticity can itself only be guaranteed if the relationship between the image and its source is rid of either the plurality or overdetermination, potential or actual, that will jeopardise the work of homology; ie repetition of the same within the reign of the Same.

Even having moved from repetition structured within the terms set by the Same and thus which demand a repetition that is the same, to a dynamic repetition, presentations still occur. In broad terms it remains the case that there is still a giving. However there is a different occurrence, for what is given now is the affirmed presence of the same and different (presence as that copresence marking the complex simultaneity of the event). The introduction of an event whose plurality is marked by irreducibility becomes part of the work of the reworking of repetition. Moreover the positing of this irreducibility alludes to, perhaps even invokes, the threat that was always inherent in the interarticulation of image and mimesis. Here beyond the range of this threat and thus the work of identity and the repetition of, and in, the same — the deferral of its reign — there is the redolent presence of the poem *Todesfugue*; sounding repetition.

The place and work of repetition will mean that Celan's poem can be provisionally described as the enactment of a repetition working within the abeyance of similitude and thus beyond the sway of the domination of the Same. Its being that enactment means that is eschews firstly any straightforward formulation of the logic of identity and secondly any rigid distinction between form and content. It opens at that precise point. The poem thus demands, both within and as the act of interpretation, that the question of identity and the stakes of repetition come to be reposed. They can no longer be taken as given. (Delaying the impact of the given is not a move that would occur prior to interpretation nor would it be a prelude; on the contrary, it emerges as part of the act of interpretation itself.) It is this demand which figures here both in terms of the problem of citation and the subsequent location of that problem within the frame. The citation becomes a repetition of the site of repetition; its being given within and for questioning. The difficulty arises here not from having to provide a formulation for the relationship between the line and the poem but from the location of the line within and as part of the painting. As a beginning it is a part of the painting while being, at the same time, because of its generic place, apart from it.

Provisionally, Celan's poem situates a contrast between two forces; two moments that become history. One is marked by the name Margarete and the other by the name Shulamite. The Margarete named in the title of painting, as in the poem, is the presence of Germany. Margarete is contrasted with Shulamite whose hair is ashes — 'dein aschens Haar Shulamith' (this line becomes the title of another painting of this period). Shulamite figures the Jew. The confrontation within the poem between Germany and the Jew, a confrontation mediated by the Shoah, is rehearsed in the frame. It is these two names which are present as either titles or figure as a part of what is framed within a number of Kiefer's paintings undertaken in 1981. The complexity of the proper name emerges at the moment when what is taken as central is the question of the named's ontology (the ontology of referent) and where that question is then allowed to reflect onto the given singularity of the name; in the end, of course, the putative singularity. As the work of these proper names indicates, the proper name has a specific and unique referent on the condition that what it names is never just a singular and unique referent. The propriety of the proper name is maintained to the extent that it enjoins a type of paradox; again paradox as the appearance, thus also the presence of irreducibility. From the moment they are at work within the poem and in the paintings the presence of proper names raises the complex question of what they name. The complexity is reinforced once it is recognised that as names they also function as titles. It is thus that here the proper name not only attests to the presence of an ineliminable doubling — a primordial plurality within naming — it also affirms that presence.

Within the poem what the names mark out is only fixed in repetition. If one is the figure of Germany and the other is the figure of the Jew then such a description only works if these figures are understood as an integral part of the poem's rhythm. At first the names are contrasted, then in the final two lines they abut. What they do not form is an integrated whole. Their irreducibility figures in the poem in terms of the oppositions between life and death, and then, between solidity and smoke. It is also present in the contrast between 'golden hair' and 'ashen hair'. In other words their presence — present within repetition — eschews both mediation and indifference. Synthesis and singularity are distanced and reworked. The names Margarete and Shulamite enjoin relations because of the impossibility of any consideration of the history of Germany independently of the Shoah. (Dating only establishes the borders in which a reworking of the 'given' takes place.[9]) And yet the Shoah remains as the event that works to check all events because of its singularity. A singularity that in being maintained and thus repeated works to open that singularity beyond itself. It is thus that the contrast and inseparability of Shulamite and Margarete means that to the extent that they are apart they form a part. It is precisely in terms of the apart/a part that the words forming part of what is framed as well as the combination of oil, straw and emulsion can be understood. The latter is not just the presence of mixed media. As will be seen it signals a more significant and radical division within the frame. Furthermore, while paintings such as *Your Golden Hair, Margarete — Midsummer Night* and *Margarete* do not incorporate either the figure or the name of Shulamite, she is there in the burnt straw, or in the dark and ashen markings. Her presence does not demand representation. The interplay of these two figures is captured in an important way in *Your Golden Hair, Margarete.* Looking at how this works will open a way towards the words in the frame. The words are, in addition, the title. Again the title figures as that which names the site of anoriginal complexity.

In its most simple presentation this painting is a landscape; the furrows depicting the field move towards, and away from, the painted horizon. On one side is a group of houses. The juxtaposition works to reinforce the presence of golden straw and large black marks. One of the latter is applied in such a way that it borders the straw. The reciprocal description would of course also be true. Before moving on in this description, it is essential to note that the problem of representation and how history can be represented forms a vital part of Kiefer's project. It is a project that is depicted and projected, in and as painting. The landscape is the field of history. It is the inscription of the place of history into the painting, and as painting. If history is not just the recitation of events, then the presence of the field is Kiefer's response to the question of how the event of history is to be represented; history as the field of repetition — a repetition that breaks within the dominance of the Same by the repetition of landscape where that repetition is contemporaneous with the impossibility of the field's being reduced to a simple enactment, repetition, within the genre of landscape. The frame becomes therefore the field of irreducibility and thus the site of anoriginal heterogeneity. The frame resists simplicity.

The straw and the black marks are part of what is framed, are part of the furrows in that they cross them and yet are apart from the furrows. Again, the straw is part of the painting's work and yet it is neither painted nor is it paint. Its presence complicates the canvas. A complication identified once the straw is understood as more than a simple addition. (Thinking addition beyond simple addition involves taking up the presence of complexity.) The straw plays an integral role but only on the condition that it is not, in any sense of the term, part of painting. Its presence is enacted within the logic of the apart/a part. The straw and the black marks do not have representation or even symbolic force in terms of themselves but only in relation to the words. They do not in any straightforward sense therefore either represent or function as symbols. The words work to inscribe the concerns of Celan's poem into the painting, as part of the painting, such that the relation that is thereby established between all the elements within the frame works to picture the copresence of Germany and its other within the field of history. The Germany in question is not an element of a tradition that can be denied or displaced. Not only is this rendered impossible by the interplay of apart/a part, it is also marked by the furrows, the place.

They designate the field of renewal. However the site of renewal is not new; it is the working over of what is given. Renewal, in this sense, is not the new but the copresence of the again and the anew. There cannot be one without the other. It is the line, in opening a field of repetition by introducing the play of repetition, that drives the work of the painting. The words, in being a part yet apart, also open the possibility of a presence that eschews the distinction between the literal and the figural, and thus displaces by reincorporating — reworking as reincorporation — the strategies of representation and mimesis. What is at stake, therefore, in this specific painting is the image beyond the image; painted words.

With Kiefer's paintings — or at least the paintings taken up here — the place of history, rather than having been deployed as either a given or refused as impossible, is presented as an already ineliminably present concern. The nature of the concern, however, is neither abstract nor complacent. Representation — its conditions of possibility — becomes the site of an investigation and a thinking (a painterly thinking) that takes place from within the process of presentation itself. Once more this needs to be understood as a claim that takes as central the repositioning of the object in terms of the becoming-object, and thus with the object being maintained as the object-in-question.

*Anselm Kiefer*, Dein goldenes Haar, Margarethe (Your Golden Hair, Margarete), *1981, oil, acrylic, emulsion, charcoal, straw on burlap, 130x170cm (reproduced courtesy of the artist)*

# Notes

## Introduction

**1** Presenting here, however, will still involve engagement. Nonetheless, while there will be engagement and thus the recognised necessity of a 'working through', its presence will for the most part be implicit. The difficulty of working with and within the ineliminable presence of the given is signalled by the reworked retention of tracking and tacking as providing the means and modality of that engagement. In the case of Ryman and Pollock a more directly engaged way in has been deployed. With Ryman this involves starting with Kant's consideration of the possible beauty of colour, and with Pollock working through that which determines the figure of Pollock in the writings of Greenberg and to a certain extent Rosenberg. In both cases the place of repetition and work remains central.

**2** This conception of tradition is clarified in the following chapter. An earlier formulation is presented in my *Art, Mimesis and the Avant-Garde* (London: Routledge, 1991), pp 108-114.

**3** The link between the 'already given' and the logic of the gift is established in my *The Plural Event* (London: Routledge, 1993). See in particular pp 10-15.

**4** While it cannot be pursued in any detail, it is worthwhile noting that chance here is not the chance that the history of philosophy counterposes to reason (Descartes) or necessity (Hegel). Here chance has another possibility. Pursuing this chance might well start with Bataille's 'La position de la chance' in his 'Sur Nietzsche' in *Œuvres Complètes VI* (Paris: Gallimard, 1973), pp 95-133. Significantly it is here that Bataille, in taking up the question of impossibility and possibility, notes the following in passing: 'L'*impossible* est levé si la lutte est possible.' [The *impossible* is lifted if the struggle is possible.] While such a note necessitates a detailed analysis that would place it in the wider context of Bataille's writings on this topic, it remains the case that what ii evokes would serve as the thread that links tracking, tacking and the distancing of the negative.

**5** The analysis of the negative here is truncated and cursory. It opens up the need for a detailed treatment of this topic. Its importance in this context, however, is provided by its allowing repetition a transformative role.

## Objects and Questions

**1** The term 'actative' will play a significant role here. It is linked to the reworking of ontology. What it refers to is the place and centrality of action. It is an already present quality within the object, and its use signals a further attempt to rework the nature of the object in terms of an ontology of becoming.

**2** Tradition is to be understood as the 'already given'. This means the conditions of possibility for meaning, understanding, experience, etc, are themselves already at play prior to any one act that can be taken as falling under these headings. It goes without saying that there is a complexity within tradition. There is both the presence of the marginal as well as the dominant within tradition. Moreover the activity of interpretation — an activity understood here as articulated within the varying and, in the end, differential modalities of repetition — will allow, in one of its determinations, a reworking and thus repositioning of the given such that the departure from the 'already given' becomes part of the activity of interpretation.

**3** A distinction is being drawn here between a metaphysical conception of destruction and destruction's other possibility. I have analysed the former of these in *The Plural Event*, tracing the work of this type of destruction in the writings of Descartes and Heidegger. Part of what is being developed here is the other destruction. The necessity of reworking destruction lies in allowing for the possibility of that act whose coming to presence enacts the sundering of the Same's repetition.

**4** For an important overview of some of the issues that arise once modernity and hence the postmodern are taken up as elements within a philosophical consideration of historical time, see Peter Osborne, 'Modernity is a Qualitative, not a Chronological Category', *New Left Review*, 192, March/April 1992.

**5** The possibility of this release is thought by Walter Benjamin in terms of redemption. I have tried to link Benjamin's concerns to a philosophical thinking that takes repetition and ontology as central in 'Time and Task: Benjamin and Heidegger Showing the Present', in A Benjamin and P Osborne (eds), *Walter Benjamin's Philosophy* (London: Routledge, 1994).

**6** For a detailed treatment of this use of Freud see *The Plural Event*, pp 181-7.

**7** I have tried to argue for this position in greater detail in 'Distancing and Spacing' in *Art, Mimesis and the Avant-Garde*.

**8** The implicit distinction at work here is between two fundamentally different locations of truth. With regard to representation, the truth content of the object is provided by its subject matter; for example, the narrative content of the painting. With this location the question of the object remains unposed. Once there is a move to the becoming-object, then the truth of the object — assuming that such an expression is still apposite — refers to the object's being. The locus of interpretation will involve the complex interplay between the becoming-object and that which is given — the occurrence — to be interpreted.

### Matter and Meaning: On Installations and Sites

**1** This chapter incorporates parts of an earlier attempt to give a philosophical description of the installation. See 'Matter and Meaning' in *Art and Design*, Vol 9, No 1/2, 1993.

**2** What is being gestured at here is that if the determination of chronology and genre are not taken as proving an interpretive and historical *fait accompli*, then part of what constitutes the present is the conflict over its nature. Accepting this as a point of departure will reposition terms such as 'modernity' and the 'contemporary'.

**3** What is designated as the sphere of art is not intended to address, as yet, the existence of the art object as such. Indeed, it has already been suggested that the only adequate way in which that question can be addressed is in terms of a reworking of the object as the becoming-object and, equally, the object-in-question.

### Material Events: Langlands & Bell

**1** This chapter takes up and develops an earlier attempt to write on the work of Langlands & Bell in 'Material Events: The Work of Langlands & Bell', *Art and Design*, Vol 6, No 3/4, 1990.

**2** Here what is identified as the 'already given' needs to be understood as the work of tradition. For a more detailed account of tradition see note 2 of Chapter 1.

**3** This conception of the event has been presented in greater detail in *The Plural Event*.

**4** Extract from an unpublished interview with Glen Scott Wright.

**5** Rather than the work having either a prescriptive quality or its being no more than that which attests to art's negative place, here the actual nature of the engagement — engagement as working through the given — has a displacing function that reveals the essential determinations of tradition's work. By developing this site it would become possible to reposition art's critical possibility.

**6** This formulation is given in an interview with Adrian Dannatt published as 'Langlands & Bell: Architecture as Logo', *Flash Art*, November/December, 1991.

**7** In the initial presentation of this point (in the article cited in note 1) it was formulated in terms of the logic of the again and the anew. Both that logic and what has been formulated here in terms of the apart/a part are ways of developing an affirmative conception of the new and thus of allowing for the possibility of a repetition in which what takes place occurs again for the first time. In any attempt to work through the already given there will be the inevitable problems of formulation and vocabulary.

**8** Marie-Ange Brayer on Langlands & Bell: 'Temporal Logography'. This essay was published in the catalogue *Surrounding Time*, Fonds Regional d'Art Contemporain du Centre, Orléans, France, 1993.

**9** Further consideration of the interplay between modernism, formalism and beauty is undertaken in Chapter 5 in relation to the paintings and thus the work of Robert Ryman.

### Installed Memory: Christian Boltanski

**1** Part of what is involved in allowing 'today' to play a determining role in philosophical thinking is that it acknowledges the necessity to have a philosophical conception of the present. Even in allowing historical occurrences a determining role in the present, such determinations still demand to be thought philosophically. In the case of the Shoah — and this will be in part what gives it its complex singularity — it has to play a determining role in its own being thought. The Shoah brings philosophical thinking to the brink of that possibility where parts of its own make-up as a body of thought will be implicated in the Shoah, while other parts will be unable to think — to respond by thinking — the nature of the occurrence itself. For a discussion of how these issues are at work within the project of writing history see Charles S Maier, *The Unmasterable Past. History, Holocaust and German National Identity* (Cambridge, Mass: Harvard University Press, 1988).

**2** In this instance tragedy has the minimal definition of a conflict — a conflict inescapably linked to life and death — that is necessarily irresolvable in the terms in which it is presented. Here, rather than life and death being literal, they function as the figural presence of a fundamental irresolvability. The lack of resolution however is not the consequence of a founding conflict but rather of a now absent possibility.

**3** Philippe Lacoue-Labarthe's elaboration of what is intended by the term 'massacre' is developed in the context of his more general argument that attempts to show that Western metaphysics is itself implicated in the Holocaust. See *La Fiction du Politique* (Paris: Christian Bourgois, 1987). Lacoue-Labarthe's essentially Heideggerian argument — an argument that utilises Heidegger against Heidegger — could be read in conjunction with Zygment Bauman's *Modernity and the Holocaust* (Oxford: Polity, 1989). The latter attempts to locate the Holocaust within and as inseparable from the development of modernity.

**4** Emil Fackenheim, *To Mend the World* (New York: Schocken Books, 1989), p 310.

**5** Michael Newman, 'Suffering from Reminiscences' in F Barker, P Hulme and M Iversen (eds), *Postmodernism and the Re-reading of Modernity* (Manchester: Manchester University Press, 1992). While what had been offered here is a critical engagement with Newman's work, it nonetheless must be acknowledged that his paper offers what is probably the most philosophically and politically informed interpretation of Boltanski and Kiefer to date. The disagreement is significant precisely because of the importance of Newman's work.

**6** Ibid, p 104.

**7** Ibid.

**8** Ibid.

**9** For an overview of the nature of the division between orthodoxy and reform Judaism that takes the context of differing responses to modernity as essential, see M Gillis, 'The Troubled Heart of Jewish Unity' in *The Jewish Quarterly*, No 152, Winter 1993/4. Gillis is responding to the argument put forward by Jonathan Sacks in *One People? Tradition, Modernity and Jewish Unity* (Oxford: Oxford University Press, 1993).

**10** *Republic*, 514-520. While this passage demands considerable analysis and should be linked to the way in which truth and light figure within the history of philosophy, its significant moments will be the link established by Descartes between truth and 'clear and distinct perception', and the fundamental significance accorded to light and truth by Heidegger in 'On the Essence of Truth' and 'Time and Being'.

**11** Lynn Gumpert, 'The Many Faces of Christian Boltanski' in *Reconstitution*, Whitechapel Gallery, London, 1990.

**12** For a sustained philosophical analysis of mass death see E Wyschogrod, *Spirit in Ashes: Hegel, Heidegger and Man-Made Mass Death* (New Haven: Yale University Press, 1985).

**13** It is clear that any discussion of the face will automatically be indebted to the work of Levinas. Perhaps the most important text in this regard is *Totalité et Infini* (The Hague: Martinus Nijhoff, 1984). See in particular pp 168-195.

**Painting as Object: Robert Ryman**

**1** The approach of this chapter involves working through Kant's treatment of colour in the *Critique of Judgement*. In sum, the point of such an approach is the following: with minimalism and the monochromatic canvas there would seem to be the possibility of a pure and thus simple object. Fulfilling those conditions would mean that such an object is enacted the way in which colour for Kant could be beautiful. However, the reason why there cannot be simplicity for Kant and therefore why Kant cannot, in the end, eliminate anoriginal complexity will be the same as that which causes the minimal object to deny simplicity and therefore mark out, in its simplicity, the presence of this founding complexity. Working through Kant therefore will work to open up the move from possibility to impossibility in Ryman. However, Ryman's work is not the simple negation of the beautiful. It is rather that his work traces the consequence of the recognition of the impossibility of a founding purity both from the internality of painting itself to that pivotal moment in his work in which painting, from within the practice and activity of painting, explores, as an essential part of its work, painting's own relationship to sculpture.

**2** Yve-Alain Bois, 'Ryman's Tact' in *Painting as Model* (Cambridge, Mass: MIT Press, 1993), p 223.

**3** Ibid, pp 224-5.

**4** In referencing Ryman's works dates have been added where it is necessary to distinguish between different works of the same name.

**5** I Kant, *Critique of Judgement*, translated by J Bernard (New York: Hafner Press, 1951). All subsequent references by Section number in text and page number in the footnotes.

**6** I Kant, *Critique of Pure Reason*, translated by N Kemp Smith (London: Macmillan, 1969).

**7** *Critique of Judgement*, pp 59-60.

**8** Ibid, p 60.

**9** While it was always denied by Greenberg, the conjecture being advanced here is that minimalism is the logical consequence of his conception of autonomy and moreover the consequence of modernist criticism's adoption of Kant.

**10** *Critique of Judgement*, p 73.

**11** It is interesting to note in this regard that, while the type of judgement may change — logical as opposed to aesthetic — the actual structure of judgement does not.

**12** *Critique of Judgement*, p 63.

**13** Spector has in this description touched the heart of the modernist conception of minimalism and in particular Ryman's work. For her detailed analysis see the 1984 Whitechapel Gallery exhibition catalogue.

**14** Central aspects of Greenberg's work are discussed in relation to Jackson Pollock in Chapter 6.

**15** For a more detailed discussion of intentional logic see my 'Interpreting Reflections: Painting Mirrors' in *Art, Mimesis and the Avant-Garde*, in particular pp 13-4.

### Timed Surfaces: Jackson Pollock

**1** This chapter contains elements of an earlier and more programmatic paper, 'Events with Depth: Jackson Pollock's Action Paintings', *Art and Design*, Vol 5, No 11/12, 1989. Furthermore, the approach taken here differs from that undertaken in the earlier chapters. Here as a mode of approach, the criticism and thus the reception of Pollock provides the initial site of engagement. This approach has been taken for two reasons. The first is that the wealth of material on Pollock has to a certain degree constructed the figure of Pollock, and secondly that what characterises the majority of those writing is a failure to see the action paintings as an already present affirmation of the becoming-object. The denial of that status in marking the reception provides a clear way into the work of the action paintings.

**2** For a detailed formulation of the anoriginal see *The Plural Event*.

**3** It is this position which dominates, though for significantly different reasons, a range of papers on Pollock. For example Rosalind Krauss will argue that it is clear from the reception of his work that, with regard to his painting, 'we possess none of the keys essential to understanding them'. Quoted in Bois, *Painting as Model*, p 182.

**4** For an analysis of this point see Peter Osborne, 'Aesthetic Autonomy and the Crisis of Theory: Greenberg, Adorno and the Problem of the Visual Arts in Post-Modernism', *New Formations*, No 9, Winter 1989.

**5** In D Shapiro and C Shapiro (eds), *Abstract Expressionism* (Cambridge: Cambridge University Press, 1990), p 70.

**6** Greenberg in *Abstract Expressionism*, p 71.

**7** Ibid.

**8** In *Abstract Expressionism*, p 380.

**9** Osborne, 'Aesthetic Autonomy and the Crisis of Theory', p 41.

**10** Greenberg in *Abstract Expressionism*, p 71.

**11** For an exploration of the problem of the decorative within Pollock's work see Timothy Clark, 'Jackson Pollock's Abstraction' in S Guilbaut (ed), *Reconstructing Modernism* (Cambridge, Mass: MIT Press, 1990).

**12** Harold Rosenberg, 'The American Action Painters', *Art News*, December 1952.

**13** Annette Cox, *Art as Politics* (Ann Arbour: UMI Research Press, 1981), p 88.

### Placing History: Anselm Kiefer

**1** This chapter offers a sustained reworking of an earlier paper on Kiefer published as 'Kiefer's Approaches', in A Benjamin and P Osborne (eds) *Thinking Art: Beyond Traditional Aesthetics* (London: ICA Publications, 1991). Kiefer's relation to Celan still demands more detailed work.

**2** The immense significance of the Shoah for the

project of thinking is taken as a *sine qua non* in this analysis. Both Boltanski and Kiefer can be understood as artists whose work involves a systematic engagement with that significance.

**3** Paradox plays an important role here because of its link to time. The presence of the paint brush/taper as holding both possibilities maintains them at the same time. While the time is singular the attempt to narrativise it, ie to explain in descriptive and sequential terms what is taking place, would still the force of the insistent complexity. Again what is at work here is a time — a time that is an 'at the same time' — where what is marked out by the 'same' is a plural or overdetermined present. The same, in resisting singularity and unity, is never the same as itself since there will be no unified and singular 'itself'. It is thus that what is at play here can be described as paradoxical. Paradox indicates the productive presence of the event.

**4** The again/anew involves a similar logic as the apart/a part are both ways of taking up and developing a thinking of the new and thus of a disruption of the Same that involves the abeyance of metaphysical destruction.

**5** For a more detailed discussion of 'intentional logic' see 'Interpreting Reflections: Painting Mirrors', in my *Art, Mimesis and the Avant-Garde*.

**6** This position was developed with regard to the work of Langlands & Bell in Chapter 3.

**7** It is thus that the title, rather than naming either a fixed site or that which will be allowed to have an essential quality, names the already actative nature of the art work. Here the title names work in naming, in addition, the move from the substantive towards the actative.

**8** For a discussion of the role of repetition in Celan's poetry that pays particular attention to *Todesfuge* see John Felstiner. 'Translating Paul Celan's "Todesfuge": Rhythm and Repetition as Metaphor', in Saul Friedlander (ed), *Probing the Limits of Representation: Nazism and the Final Solution* (Cambridge, Mass: Harvard University Press, 1992), particularly pp 252-4; and Leonard Olschner, 'Fugal Provocation in Paul Celan's "Todesfuge" and "Engfuhrung"' , in *German Life and Letters*, 43, 1, 1989.

**9** In this regard see my article 'Shoah, Remembrance and the Abeyance of Fate: Walter Benjamin's Fate and Character' in *New Formations*, No 20, 1993.